T0122109

The changing decades of a

BABY BOOMER

A life of adventure

PETER POUNDS

© 2022 Peter Pounds. All rights reserved.

No part of this book may be reproduced, stored in a retrieval system, or transmitted by any means without the written permission of the author.

AuthorHouse™ UK
1663 Liberty Drive
Bloomington, IN 47403 USA
www.authorhouse.co.uk
UK TFN: 0800 0148641 (Toll Free inside the UK)
UK Local: 02036 956322 (+44 20 3695 6322 from outside the UK)

Because of the dynamic nature of the Internet, any web addresses or links contained in this book may have changed since publication and may no longer be valid. The views expressed in this work are solely those of the author and do not necessarily reflect the views of the publisher, and the publisher hereby disclaims any responsibility for them.

Any people depicted in stock imagery provided by Getty Images are models, and such images are being used for illustrative purposes only.
Certain stock imagery © Getty Images.

This book is printed on acid-free paper.

ISBN: 978-1-6655-9615-2 (sc)
ISBN: 978-1-6655-9614-5 (e)

Print information available on the last page.

Published by AuthorHouse 01/31/2022

authorHOUSE®

Dedication

To my long-suffering wife, Joan, who has let me go on all these adventure trips and has been invaluable in producing this book.

The changing decades of a BABY BOOMER

Introduction

On the first day back at school at Clee Grammar, Cleethorpes, the Head, Mr Shaw, started by saying, "A new year and new decade." It was Colin Shaw and it said 'C. Shaw' on his office door. Appropriate for a seaside town! This got me thinking, at the age of 14 a decade had been a lifetime. The next decade would be another lifetime. In ten years, I would have done my 'O'- and 'A'-levels, gone to college, and may be even married! Ten years – I could not comprehend it. As it happened, each decade of my life did change dramatically. 1950s, school. 1960s, Grammar school and college. 1970s, family, allotment, and weightlifting. 1980s, Open University and climbing UK. 1990s, climbing Europe. 2000s, retirement. 2010s, mountaineering worldwide. And and then 2020s, Covid! I started taking photos when I cycled over the Alps in 1964. Since then, I have amassed 7,000 slides. Forty years later, photography went digital and now I have another 10,000 or so. Therefore this little book is a photographic record of the changing decades of my life.

Contents

Chapter 1.

1950s: Post war years.

1950s: schooldays. Can't remember much. I was living in a three-bedroomed terraced house with my Mum and Dad, two older sisters Rita and Dena, my Grandad and two young uncles, Jim and Frank. No central heating, double glazing, TV, phone or car. But this was normal. On frosty mornings there was ice on the inside of the windows, as there were four of us in my room. I walked to school, as everyone did. This was Bursar Street School. Some of the buildings were temporary as during the war a bomber dropped three bombs: one hit a street away from our house; one fell opposite my school where the new building was; and the third was a direct hit on a cyclist trying to get home. It was Maurice Wharton who lived a few doors down from us. The shrapnel scars were still in the lamppost fifteen years later! The school was seven-stream entry (seven classes per year) with fifty in a class – all baby boomers after the soldiers returned after the war. My Dad was captured in North Africa by the Italians in the first phase of the disastrous campaign. Sent to Italy when the Italians capitulated, he was set free, but an Italian farmer told the Germans where they were, so they were recaptured and did a 1,000-mile march into Germany where he spent the rest of the war. When he returned, besides me being the result, he got a job in Nottingham as a wet fish shop manager. When the 1947 winter ended, the River Trent flooded the bottom floor of the shop to within six inches of the ceiling. As a toddler I was told that I used to chase my sisters around the shop with a wet cod, with my fingers in its eyes as a good hold. My sisters never liked me from the start as when my mother was about to give birth to me, she said to my sisters at dinner time, "When you come from school, I might have a surprise for you." Of course they thought it could be chocolate, which was rare at the time. Disappointingly, the surprise was me!

My family. My mother was one of eight; she had three older brothers. She was born in 1918, so they called her Gladys, as they were glad the war was over and she was the first girl. She hates the name! Her mother died of childbirth and so did the child in 1930s. My mother took over as housewife looking after her younger siblings. My father was one of seven. He was the youngest son, born in 1915. When he got to employment age, it was the great depression, so jobs were few. In 1940 he went off to war. My grandad on my mother's side was Jim Smith, a landscape gardener. He was a talented man: an artist and a craftsman who made bookcases, radios and gramophones. He drew a lot of ink portraits of several beautiful women and nobody knows who they were! At his allotment he grew the best tomatoes in the world. Only a few knew the secret. He never had a toilet at his garden so had a big bucket of fermented urine! That did the trick. He was still working at 88. When he came home he washed his soiled hands and left the soap on the side. My Mum used to complain that she had to wash the soap afterwards! I had dozens of aunts and uncles and cousins. Before anyone had cars, the whole family would cycle to Weelsby Woods on a sunny Sunday for a big picnic and to play rounders. Good days spoilt by the advent of cars. No one had a car in the 1950s. In my street only the dairyman had a car – an Austin 7. So all the kids played in the streets. Hundreds of us! We also played on 'bommies', or bombed sites, which were common, as the Luftwaffe tried to hit Grimsby docks but only killed poor old Maurice! Talking about the Luftwaffe, my Uncle Ron was a flight sergeant in the RAF. He was a tail end Charlie or rear gunner – the most dangerous place to be. He shot down a few planes and was awarded the Dinstinguished Flying Cross.

Grammar school. In 1958 I passed my 11+ and went to Clee Grammar for boys. Bullying the first year boys was traditional! Being thrown off the mound in the school field, an old air-raid shelter, was common. Boxing was also traditional and I entered the school boxing competition. My first bout was against Mick. He was the school genius, but he couldn't box. He never hit me once! In the third bout, against Stewart, I hit him with a brilliant right hook. He sat down and cried his eyes out. A technical knockout! I went on to win the final in a proper ring, but my mother wouldn't come to see me. My dad and uncle Frank came. Uncle Frank thought I'd grow up to be a bit soft, as my mother mollycoddled me. He changed his mind after that.

My dad bought me a racing bike for my next birthday – a Viking. My life was about to change. Sunday was cycling day, so it was a good excuse not to go to church. I had been confirmed in the

Church of England. In the last few years I only went to ogle at a girl called Ann on the front row. I never listened to the sermons or anything.

Our wedding day

Dad

Me as a toddler

My Grandad

Mum and Dad

Chapter 2.

1960s: Education, running, and cycling.

I had been top of the class at maths at junior school and at grammar school, but as soon as we did algebra and theorems I was lost. I realised much later that I was good at arithmetic but not maths. Also, at grammar school they expected everyone to 'get it' straight away. The only subjects I liked were geography, art and P.E. Each year we were weighed and measured. In my Encyclopaedia Britannica it listed the average height and weight of children as they grew. I was within half an inch and half a pound of average each year. It said that I would be 5 foot 9 inches and 11 stone 6 pounds when I grew up. Unfortunately, after the third year I stopped growing and all my peers overtook me. It didn't bother me as I could out-run and out-cycle everyone and was never short of a girlfriend! My cycling got me really fit, so in athletics I was good at middle- and long-distance running. I won the half-mile in record time on sports day and got my picture on the front page of the Grimsby Telegraph.

In 1961 my sister married, had a baby, and moved to Gainsborough, so I cycled there and back one Sunday. Eighty miles – my first big ride. The following year she moved to Canterbury, so me and my best mate, Pete, cycled there. A distance of 220 miles. We didn't look at weather forecasts as we didn't have a TV. We set off to Ely YHA across the fens against a force six head wind. It took us twelve hours. The next morning dawned windless and sunny, but it still took twelve hours. Back in Lincolnshire we often saw a group of cyclists. Unbeknown to me they referred to us as "Bugs and his mate". We eventually joined at Nun's corner where they met each Sunday to be greeted, "It's Bugs". So the name stuck – my first nickname of many. I was called Pancho at college and Pedro at school, as I had grown a Mexican droopy moustache. The club was called East Coast Olympic and we started racing with them. I was good on the hills as I weighed just 8 stone 7 pounds. Pete was a sprinter. October was hill climb month. Nobody in the club had a car, so we rode to the events on a double-sided fixed wheel. At Ruckland hill we changed the wheel around for a lower gear. Ruckland was 660 yards with an average gradient of ten per cent, steepest incline was seventeen per cent. I won it in 1 minute and 30 seconds: that's fifteen miles per hour uphill! The next week our team cycled to the ferry across the Humber – a paddle steamer. Then fourteen miles west to Brantingham hill climb. Headwind all the way. I won it by six seconds, and nearly caught my minute man. We also won the team prize, me Pete and Dave. Then we cycled the forty miles back home. We thought nothing of it. I wish I could do it now. In 1964 I set off to cycle to Land's End via my Uncle Ron's in Glossop, Wales, North Devon (up Porlock Hill with a twenty per cent gradient), to Penzance. I popped to Land's End in the evening. Then back over Dartmoor, Dorset, and back through the Midlands. Twelve days youth hostelling. I stopped at Litton Cheney Youth Hostel, where I had stayed the previous year. The Warden remembered me. I kept in touch and became his assistant warden for five years. Whilst all this cycling was going on, I was running for school, but it was the cycling that kept me fit. I was doing over 5,000 miles a year. In the winter we used to cycle to the Peak District to get some miles in as well as some long hills: 100 miles on Saturday, Youth Hostel, and back on Sunday. I did it once by myself. At the Youth Hostel there was a school girls' group who tried to attract my attention, but I was very shy at the time and never took advantage. I did learn later, however. I won the school cross country in the third year (Year 9 now) and set records in the 880 yards and the mile. In the fourth year we were allowed to run the mile. My first mile race was against Wintringham Grammer. They had a good runner called Harry. "You'll not beat him," they said. He set off like a hare and took thirty yards on me. After one lap he was still thirty yards ahead. Half a lap to go and I was on his shoulder. I sprinted past him in the last 100 yards and beat him by five seconds. He said, "I'll beat you at the Inter Grammar." The highlight of the year was the inter grammar champs held at RAF Cranwell, the only cinder track in the county. As we gathered to start, I looked worried and Mr Roberts, my P.E. teacher asked what was wrong. I said, "They're all bigger than me sir." I was 5 foot 5 inches. He said, "Just burn a hole in the track, Pounds." They went so slow in the first lap, so with two-and-three-quarters of a lap to go, I sprinted into the lead and won by 100 yards in record time – 4 minutes 40 seconds. I got my athletics colours for that and the Goodwin memorial cup for athletics on prize day. Harry said he'd beat me at the county champs. Three weeks later I won that too. County champ! I was always late for school when my form teacher said 'Pounds' at registration,

I was in the hall being told I was winning this trophy. Cess, our form teacher, said, "I suppose he's late again." My friend said, "No, he's in the hall. He's getting a prize."

"Pounds? getting a prize? For what?"

"Athletics Sir."

"Oh," he said.

Cess was my French teacher and I was no good at French. 1963 was 'O'-level year. I actually passed French, much to the astonishment of Cess and myself. I opted to do geography, history, and art at 'A'-level, which I passed. I won a place at Enfield to do a degree in geography, history and economics. I hated it, so I applied to Portsmouth and Kingston to study geology, my favourite subject. I had been collecting fossils from Cleethorpes for years. But I needed Latin, which I had failed the year before. Both universities wanted me, so I took Latin lessons in the evening. I was crap at French, but worse at Latin. As before, I failed again by one grade. So I applied and got in at Borough Road teaching college in Isleworth. Before I went, two friends of mine, Zac and Dave, cycled to the South of France. To earn some money for the trip I worked as a chippy's labourer at Immingham docks. One of the men was reshafting a hammer and a metal splinter flew into my leg. I didn't realise anything had happened until I felt that my leg was wet. I rolled my jeans up to find I was bleeding. I thought I'd been shot. I hobbled to first aid, was bandaged up and sent to hospital.

I asked the doctor, "Is it still in my leg?"

He replied, "Is there a hole the other side?"

"No."

"Well, it's still in there then!"

"Are you going to take it out," I asked.

"Nope, it'll work its way out in time."

I was cycling to France in ten days, with a bit of stainless steel in my leg! With only three weeks of holiday we cycled to Paris and caught the Mistral train to Marseilles. Then along the Cote d'Azur, through St. Tropez and Monte Carlo. Then north to the Alps, via the Col de la Bonette at 2,800 metres, the Col du Vars, Col d'Izoard, Col de Lautaret, and Col du Galibier. All major Cols in the Tour de France. We even passed Jaques Anquetil's house on the way. Our hero. To this day the bit of steel has not emerged!

Borough College, 1966 to 1969. This was the best college in the country for running. We even beat Loughborough College, which had more students than us. Mr Biddle never liked me, as in the interview he asked me my mile time. I said 4 minuntes 30 seconds. He said, "Huh, my boys are doing 4 minutes 12!" We had internationals and Olympic medalists in the P.E. department. Alan Pascoe won the 400 metre hurdles at the Mexico Olympics. After an athletics career winning lots of races, I never won one in three years at college. I got seconds and thirds, but never won. One winter I was entered to the East of England Cross Country champs. That's all counties from Lincolnshire to Essex. I came seventh, which I thought was good. When I got back to college they asked how I got on. When I told them they just said, "Oh." This not winning put me off running for ten years, because I liked to win! I did do well in gymnastics however, as I was more of a gymnast's build. I had built some upper body strength through weight training and weighed a whopping 9 stone 2 pounds. I became one of the best gymnasts in the year. We had to do all sports and became qualified in several. I ended up as a qualified football referee, middle distance coach, swimming teacher, and gymnastic coach. We all spent two weeks in Wales on Outdoor Pursuits – walking, climbing, canoeing, sailing, and campcraft, which would come in useful in later years. In 1969 we went skiing in Austria. This, I realised, is the stuff I want to do, as team sports never interested me.

Teaching. I got a post at Bordeston Boys school in Brentford, London. Only two stream entry. I was their first P.E. teacher. Two of the staff managed a football and cricket team and the Head took tennis. They had a gym, so I introduced basic gymnastics and keep fit. They also had a field next to a canal, so I started cross country, athletics, and canoeing. I also got a part time job at a swimming club, coaching the kids. The other coach was a big drinker and I ended up in the pub two nights a week drinking Guinness. I drove him home one night and met his wife and sister, who was visiting. His wife was very good looking with a nice figure. I was told a lot later that when I left, both his wife and sister had said, "Oh, he's a bit of alright!" They lived in a scruffy flat with their two young kids and he treated her badly. I was in love! I had an affair and he found out, but Joan and I kept in touch secretly.

My sisters Rita and Dena

Uncle Ron

National Hill Climb

Me winning sports day 880 yards

Me receiving Athletics cup

Col du Vars

Chapter 3.

1970s: Marriage, family, weight-lifting, and mountaineering.

I resigned from Bordeston as I couldn't afford to live in London on a teacher's pathetic salary. I returned to Cleethorpes and got a teaching post at Elliston Secondary as Head of Geography, with a bit of P.E. – the reverse of Bordeston. On 12 October I hired a van and went to Ealing and spirited away Joan and the two kids, Dawn and Jon, to a house I had bought in Grimsby. My life changed in an instant. Joan's husband came to visit his daughter a few times but gave up. When he was returning her to Joan after a visit, Dawn said to her mum, "Is Daddy home?," meaning me. We never saw him again. 1970 ended badly for me, as on 16 December, my dad died of cancer.

The biggest change in my life and the best was when I taught at Elliston Street Secondary School, which was near Grimsby docks. Fishing was the main industry here. So we had a lot of trawlermen's families which were big and notorious for being 'hard'. One pupil's father was a skipper on a seine netter, or 'snibby', as they were called in Grimsby. They are Danish vessels and had only a four-man crew. One summer holiday this lad went on a fishing trip with his dad. He was excited about it. Next time I saw him I asked how he got on. It was hard, he said. First day they tied him to the mast for twelve hours and put fish giblets down his trousers and he wet himself as he was there all day. When he went to bed, they had put a live crab in his sleeping bag! The men spent three weeks away and on return spent four days in the pub. The cane was used regularly to keep order.

Now a father of two with a housekeeping wife, we were poor, as teachers' salaries were £100 per month and the mortgage was £33. I taught swimming lessons twice a week at adult education and got an allotment to grow vegetables and soft fruit. I also worked on the Christmas post, at Bird's Eye in the pea season in summer, and laboured for my uncle Frank, who was a builder. Every young teacher at the time had a part-time job just to survive. Labourers were paid more than teachers! The school took kids to the Lake District each year, so I volunteered to take over. There were no restrictions then, so I started my Mountain Leadership log book so I could qualify as a mountain leader. For the next seven years I led parties to the Lakes, Wales, Dorset, Devon, and Scotland. Fell walking in the Lakes, water sports in Devon, geography trips in Dorset, and skiing in France and Scotland. To keep fit, as I wasn't running, I took up Olympic weightlifting. I was soon county champion and then divisional champion. I was in the top ten lifters in the country in Olympic and power lifting. I lifted at Bantam weight and then Featherweight as I gained five kilograms of muscle. At 60 kilograms bodyweight, my Olympic total for two lifts was 190 kilograms, and for the three power lifts, 570 kilograms. The 190 kilograms allowed me to compete at a national level. In 1973, we decided to increase the family and move to a bigger house. We moved into a big, four-bedroomed Victorian house which needed a lot of work. When Joan was nine months pregnant a teaching mate, Dave, came round to help me dig my allotment. After dinner we went to the pub. My wife said, "Don't be long." When we got back, Joan was at the door with a suitcase. "It's coming," she said. We bundled her into the car and drove to the maternity hospital, with Dave as white as a sheet. I sat at the side of the bed and within five minutes, Joan said, "Press that button." The nurses rushed around and moved her to the delivery room and then they gave me a mask and gown. "What if I feint?," I said. "Feint the other way!," was the reply. I was very brave, I thought, and didn't feint. Ann-Marie popped out in three minutes!

The school amalgamated with the Girl's Grammar School about this time to make Lindsey Comprehensive. I got a rise in salary and I started climbing with a local mountaineering group, which didn't actually climb. In 1978 I did my Mountain Leadership Certificate summer assessment in the Lake District, which lasted a week. It was in March and concentrated on navigation. First day it rained then snowed. Navigation in cloud and snow. One of the guys, Gary, got us lost and failed. We also had four written exams in the evening. On the last two days we spent a night camping at 2,500 feet in the snow. "I thought this was the summer certificate," I said to the boss, Harry.

"It is," he replied.

"Then what's this white stuff?"

By eight o'clock it was dark and very cold, so my tent mate asked if I would like some medicine. He handed me a hip flask. I drank and said, "That's good, what is it?" "Highland Park, malt whisky." I'd never drunk whisky, but after that I was hooked. Despite drinking on the job, I passed as mountain leader, summer certificate. That year we had a school ski trip to Romania, where I came third in a race.

I had joined the Yorkshire Geological Society and attended its lectures. One was on volcanoes, which had always fascinated me. I talked to the speaker who gave me a contact about expeditions to Iceland with the Young Explorers Trust. I went to several meetings and then started raising money for a school trip. Local companies gave us food, like pot noodles and tinned fish. We raised money through jumble sales and so on. Eventually six sixth formers elected to go, with three staff and a past pupil who I had climbed with. We flew to Keflavik and were driven to Reykjavik, where we caught a small plane to Akureyri in the North. We flew because there are no roads across Iceland. We ascended the nearest mountain where we camped on a plateau next to the glacier we were to survey. After the survey, we went to Myvatn, or lake of flies, saw some boiling mud pools and the crack that is splitting Iceland in half. Rain water often fills the cracks and it heats up. One had warning signs saying, "Danger, temperature 60 C." But we found a cooler one in which we could bathe, as we had been camping on a glacier and it was too cold to wash. I heard people talking from the depths of this pool and realised they were German women. There was a hole in the roof of this rock structure, so I climbed to see that, as I suspected, they were skinny dipping. One of them heard us and said, "Come on in. Don't be shy." We didn't need a second invitation! The water was bath-temperature and very salty, but it was the first bath for two weeks. We also visited Strokkur, the geyser that erupts every five minutes. Back in Reykjavik, we went to a pub, but could only afford one drink. Beer was seven pounds a pint even then! The country is fantastic, but expensive.

After my MLC and Iceland I decided to try a winter mountaineering course at Glenmore Lodge near Aviemore, Scotland. A week in the snow, on the Cairngorms. After three days I still hadn't seen them as we were always in cloud. We built snow shelters, practised ice climbing and ice axe braking: on our backs feet first, on out fronts feet first, on our fronts head first and on our backs head first. The last one is terrifying. Then two days camping out at 4,000 feet, without a tent. So, we dug a snow hole. My partner had just spent two years in the Antarctic, so was at home with snow. After two hours we had an ice palace in which we could stand up. It had shelves. The boss put his head in and said, "This is a big place, lads. The two girls have only got in two feet and it's dark in an hour. Could you take one in?" I had promised my wife not to share a snow hole with a woman, but we had to take one in, so we plumped for the quiet one. The boss had said on day one that mountains in winter "were for men". "I'll say no more," he said. "Just wait. They had previously panicked when ice bouldering." After completing the course, I decided not to get qualified as winter in the hills is too dangerous to take kids and too expensive to kit them out. There are too many objective dangers such as avalanche and frost bite. We were close to an avalanche when digging our snow hole.

Me winning school
X – Country Race

Me doing handstand

My family, Joan, Dawn,
Jon and Ann-Marie

Ann-Marie in my
climbing boots

Chapter 4.

1980s: Marathon, rock and ice climbing, Open University.

Before I started climbing a lot, I decided to finish weightlifting, as I was now a veteran of thirty-five! I had achieved national standard at Featherweight, with 82.5 kilograms snatch and 107.5 clean and jerk. Featherweight is 60 kilograms. I was invited to lift twice at the national championships and came third twice. Quite a few competitors were on steroids, but I wasn't into taking drugs for sport. I finished at 107.5 kilograms. The guy who won started his first lift at 130 kilograms!

In 1980 the Queen opened the Humber Bridge which, at the time, was the longest single span in the world. A marathon race over it was planned, so I went to watch it. I saw several old runners and cyclists that I knew running it, so I decided to start running again and beat them next year. I trained for eight months, doing sixty miles a week and aimed for a sub-three-hour time. It was Hull to Grimsby, which is north to south. There was a force six southerly wind! All the runners said it would take fifteen mins off your time. I set off with the leaders and at five miles I was at thirty-two-and-a-half minutes, which I thought was too fast. Then there was an uphill section into Barton. At each five-mile mark I was still under three-hour pace. Even at twenty miles I was okay. But at twenty-two miles I started to slow down and couldn't do anything about it. I finished in three hours and fifty-two seconds! I came 48th, out of 3,000, but was disappointed at my time. I never competed in a race again. It was time for a non-competitive sport, like climbing.

Each February half term I booked a hut in Glencoe to winter climb. There were usually six of us and we did many routes in Glencoe and Nevis. There are three major ridges on the Ben: Castle, Tower, and North East Buttress. Castle is the easiest at Grade Two, but when I did it, there were lots of red spots at the bottom of the gully. It was blood! The previous day two blokes were avalanched and killed. Near the top of North East Buttress, just past the Mantrap – a notorious rock barrier across the ridge – I was belaying Paul and the rope suddenly stopped, so I guessed he was looking for a belay. We were in the cloud and everything was white. The rock was covered in rime frost, which looked like feathers. On the ridge there was empty space – below me, to the right, to the left, and above me. I was in a featureless white world and as there was no wind, it was eerily silent. My mind wandered. I could be anywhere in the universe. I could be inside a ping pong ball! Then the rope moved and a voice shouted, "On belay. Taking in." I was back on Earth! Tower Ridge is 2,000 feet high and much has been written about it. It is Grade Three and easy up to the Eastern Traverse. I remember reading that several people had fallen off here and died on the end of the rope as it is overhanging and nobody could get to them in time. In summer the traverse is a two-feet-wide path. In winter it covered in deep snow. So many people had climbed it that season and had put their ice axes in the snow that the ice axe holes were solid and safe as houses. So it was easy and nothing to worry about. Another problem here was that it was so busy. We had to wait an hour in a queue to do it! Once past it, there was one more obstacle – the Douglas Gap. It is only six foot wide and if it was at ground level you would jump it. But up there, if you missed it, it is a 1,000-foot drop. People have been blown off here! You have to climb down into the ten-foot gap and climb up the other side. With a rope on it's fine. As there were so many people up there, we got to the summit in the dark. Head torches on, we set off on a compass bearing which offers a safe corridor between the cliffs and Five Finger Gully. After five minutes we joined another group and then another; all in line following the compass. Suddenly we were out of the cloud and we could see the lights of Fort William below. A big cheer went up! We descended Number Four Gully, which would take us to the C.I.C. hut. It's a two-hour walk out in the daylight, so longer at night. By the time we reached the car, we had a dilemma. If we went home and cooked tea, it would be closing time at the Onicht Hotel bar. So one car went back to get tea started and the others went to a Fort William off-licence to buy a load of beer. Sorted!

In Glencoe we did many climbs in Stob Coire nan Lochan, Buachaille Etive Mor, Lost Valley, and we did the Aonach Eagach ridge twice. The latter means 'notched ridge' in Gaelic. It very narrow in places.

Some bits just a foot wide. It is also almost impossible to get off it until you reach the other end. Paul and I climbed Great Gully on Buachaile Mor only a few weeks after completing our winter training. This mountain is at the head of Glencoe after you cross Rannoch Moor. It is a beautiful conical mountain. The route was supposed to be 500 feet of ice and 1,500 feet of snow, but it was a lean year for snow, so it was the other way around, with 1500 feet of ice At the bottom the water was flowing under the ice and when you put your axe in, the water leaked out. Further up, the ropes began to freeze and the belay plate wouldn't work. So, we had to do body belays. A few days later we tried Parallel D Gully, which wasn't really a gully. It was 1,000 feet and about eight pitches. In the guide book it mentioned a 100-foot iced slab – the crux. The ice was only an inch thick, so ice screws would not work. The ice covered the rock, so pitons were useless. That meant no protection, or 'no gear' as we would say. We both secretly hoped the other would get the crux pitch. As I got to Paul's belay he said, "You've got it." I raced up it on pure adrenalin. I reached a small rock corner sticking out of the ice and could see a belay thirty feet away. "How much rope left?," I shouted. "Ten feet," was the reply. "What! I need thirty ★★★★ing feet!," I screamed. "Tough, that's all you've got!," was the reply. There was a vertical crack in front of me, filled with ice. I scaped it out with my axe. I tried every piton. None would fit. I was left with a small Moac wedge. One way was far too large, the narrow way was a millimetre too wide. I had nothing else. I had run out 140 feet with no protection. A fall here would take me 140 feet to Paul and 140 feet past him! One ice axe has an adze at the other end, the second axe has a hammer. I hammered the Moac in until it was welded into the crack. I yelled for Paul to climb but added, "Don't ★★★★ing fall off." Luckily, he didn't. On the descent gully we saw a bum-shaped groove going down the mountain. Somebody had glissaded it. So we took our crampons off, sat down, and zoomed down on our backsides and descend 1,000 feet in ten minutes. Better than walking!

One year we met Andy in Glencoe. Andy was a coal miner from Barnsley. He was 'on the sick' as he was recovering from a broken leg from an accident in the Alps. He was camping in winter! We were staying in a warm hut in Glencoe, so we offered a meal that evening. He turned up and ate everything, then went to the toilet and said, "Hey, you've got a bath. Can I borrow a towel and soap and have a bath?" Afterwards we went to the Onicht Hotel for a beer or two. I was reading an ecology book. Andy asked why. I said I was doing an ecology degree as I wanted to widen my teaching scope. He told me that he had left school with no qualifications and went down the pit. When the miners went on strike, he went climbing and not on picket duty. He loved it so much he dreaded going 'downt'pit' on the Monday. So, I said, why not go to night school and get some 'O'-levels? I met him some years later and he had passed an 'A'-level as well. In English, which was a surprise as he spoke Barnsley! He went on to do his masters and PhD on the Barnsley accent and words. He has since written two books on his climbing around the world. One of Andy's climbing friends from Barnsley was a nurse called John. He had a thick accent and when relating a climbing story to one of my friends he said, "I were climbing this crack and I only had one friend [a camming device] in and it were aif in aif art."

"What? This friend, it was what?"

"Aif in aif art," he repeated.

In translation he meant, half in and half out!

I winter climbed in Scotland every February until 1989. In that year there was little snow and the summit just had a dusting on it! A few years before I had taken a sixth form group to Skye and climbed on the Cuillin Ridge. On the way back we walked up Ben Nevis and on the summit plateau there was three feet of snow – in August.

In 1983 I started an Open University course to do ecology. It was hard work fitting in a degree course whilst working, climbing, managing my allotment, and raising a family. But it was interesting and I enjoyed summer school at Nottingham, Stirling, Durham, and Malham Tarn field centre. I passed and this led to promotion at school. In 1984 I decided to go on a rock instructor's course at Plas y Brenin centre in north Wales. There was one instructor to two students. We did sea traverses, abseiling, rescue work, and climbed on several types of rock. When leading on Grim Wall, Tremadoc, I said to my instructor, "Shall I put some more gear in?" He said, "No, it's okay. Just jump off, you'll see." I put more gear in and didn't jump off. At the end of my course he said I was a competent climber and okay to teach it, but there was no certificate in those days.

To increase my scope in climbing I went to Chamonix in the Alps in 1986 with a past pupil, Tony, who was a good climber and now a junior doctor. We did a few 1-000-foot rock climbs at HVS standard, crossed glaciers, and did a lot of drinking. To save money we bivouacked at 6,000 feet, sleeping under boulders, as the cable car was quite expensive.

The year of 1989 was epic. I had been taking school children camping and climbing every summer. I also took them to Outward Bound at Eskdale each year. This is a magic place and I took the best kids every year. One day we went to do the Dalegarth Leap. This meant standing on the dry stone wall on a small bridge, over the River Esk. As you looked down, it was seventeen feet to the river which was twenty feet deep. So, from eye level to the bottom, it was forty-five feet. All the kids were watching as I gulped, so I stepped quickly before I changed my mind. I went so often that the boss put me with the new instructors as I had been on more courses than them. One night was a bivouac, but rooky instructor had booked the bivvy site too late and got a wood next to a stream. It was full of midges! I buried my head in my sleeping bag, but it was too hot. I put my head out and got bitten. I looked at my watch. It was eleven o'clock. I'll never sleep! I realised we were only two miles from the centre, so I crept out and walked back to the centre in the dark. I crept in, set my alarm on my watch, and went to sleep. Up at seven o'clock, I crept back to the bivvy site, got a stove going, made two coffees and nudged the instructor from his sleep. "Morning Roger," I said. "Want a coffee?" "Thanks, Pete. You're a star." I never told him the truth!

Summer camp. I asked the Head if I could start a summer camp for years seven, eight, and nine in July, as the fifth and sixth forms were doing exams and I was on half time table. He agreed. Twenty-four kids and six staff went to North Lees campsite for four days of adventure. We walked, rock climbed, abseiled, potholed, orienteered, sailed, and canoed. The kids did their own cooking and had evening activities. After four days they were happy, but shattered. So were the staff! Many of these kids had never been to the Peak District before, even though it's only ninety minutes away. Some had never seen a sheep. Most had never done any of these activities before. It was good to see them overcome their fears. They thought abseiling was the scariest. We often had tears going over top, followed by, "Can I do it again?" We had to have a parents' meeting beforehand and the most common worry was the potholing. "When do you hear anything about potholing in the media?," I asked. "When they are drowned," was the answer. It is news as it is so rare. "Dog bites man" is not news. "Man bites dog" is. The pots we took them down never flood. The benefit for me as a teacher was that they saw me as a human, not a teacher. I wore shorts, a bandana and colourful T-shirts. A month before the first big camp I was climbing on Burbage South on a hot day. I moaned to the lads that it was in the shade and why don't we go to Burbage North in the sun. So, we moved. I tried Long Tall Sally, a climb graded at 'E1'. The gear was sketchy and at twenty feet I put in a rock number two. I fell and it held me. I tried again and fell again. This time the gear ripped out and I decked! My left foot hit soil, but my right hit rock. I had broken my heel! We were a mile from the road, so poor old Rob piggy-backed me. At Sheffield hospital, I asked the doctor if it was broken. He said, "I don't know, I'm not a doctor. I just put this white coat on!" The x-ray came back to show a triple break. I was transferred to a cottage hospital at Rivelin after one night. The weather was hot so the nurses wheeled me out into the sun. They came round with pills and I asked if it was okay to drink alcohol with the medication. They said it was okay so I asked them to get one of the four-packs in my bedside cabinet. All my mates had brought me a four-pack! After a week I was sent home and went back to school on crutches. A month later I went to camp to organise everything. The staff drove me to the crags and I managed to climb and abseil on one leg.

After three months the plaster came off. The next day I cycled fifty miles. Three days later I was climbing. Two months later I was running. Not bad after one doctor said I would never walk over uneven ground again.

Iceland group

Glenmore Lodge – snow hole

Weight lifting

Humber marathon

Winter climbing

Ice belay

Chamonix – Tony climbing

Chapter 5.

1990s: Climbing in the Mediterranean, European travel.

All the kids had left home. Dawn had had a daughter, Cheryl, in 1987 and another, Adele, in 1989. I was a Grandad at forty-one. Jon became a Dad in 1990, with Natalie. Dawn then had two boys in the next few years, Gavin and Marc. Ann-Marie was at College. In July I noticed that we had some money left in the bank. So we booked a holiday in Mallorca. Joan had never been abroad and all our family holidays had been camping in Britain – Aviemore, the Lakes, North Wales, or Dorset. It's amazing how much money you save when you have no kids! Food, electricity, and gas bills are much lower. For the first time I didn't feel poor.

The climbing also changed, as we had been to Scotland the previous two years and there was either no snow or it rained. Rob told me that climbers had started going to Spain in February, as it was warm and cheap. So we booked to go to Alicante and climb in Costa Blanca. A few weeks before we set off, one of my past pupils, nicknamed Pooh, had called round to borrow an ice axe, as it had snowed heavily and he and three mates were going to the Peak District to ice climb. I said it hasn't been cold enough to freeze the snow yet. I advised them to go to Crowden Brook to ice boulder high up in the brook, as it is at 1,800 feet and the brook should be frozen. The two older guys were more experienced and climbed the ice. Pooh and Chris, his mate, however decided to ascend a snow bank at the side of the brook. His last words were, "I think it's going to go!" It avalanched and buried them both. The other guys heard the avalanche and ran to dig them out. They found Chris and cleared his face so he could breathe and then probed with their axes to locate Pooh. It took twenty minutes to find him, an arms and ice axe length under the snow. British snow is very close to melting point and is wet and heavy. When it stops it sets like concrete and has no air spaces. Victims are crushed and asphyxiated. When they got to him, he wasn't breathing, so Tony, a junior doctor, tried for an hour with heart compression, whilst mountain rescue came. It was too late and Pooh had sadly died. Avalanche deaths in the Peak are very rare. Once in twenty years or so. His parents were devastated and unconsolable. Only a week later we went to Alicante one climber short.

For the next ten years we climbed in the Spanish sun in February. One Monday, after returning from the trip, one of my sixth formers put her hand up and asked, "Why are you brown, Sir?" I said I'd been to Spain. I said even the dustbin man had asked me.

"Where's yer bin?"

I replied I'd been to Spain.

"No, where's yer wheely bin?"

I said that I'd really been to Spain!!

There are dozens of crags in the Costa Blanca, but we gradually widened our scope to El Chorro, Mallorca, Tenerife, Corsica, Sardinia, Croatia, Turkey, Provence, and Greece. Kalymnos is now a climbing island and we now go every year.

Costa Blanca. The first four years we booked a cheap flight to Alicante and stayed in a high-rise hotel in Calpe. Everything is cheap in Spain in winter. We met an old climber, Ron James, who was retired and spent each winter in Spain. There is a gorge just outside Calpe called Mascarat, crossed by the main road. The old road ran parallel and we had read that climbers do bridge jumps from the new bridge. The next day it rained so we went to buy some cheap climbing shoes. The forecast was for rain the next day, so we asked Ron about the bridge jump. He said he would help us set it up. We discussed it at the pub, which was owned by a gay English bloke, who said he'd like to have a go! 150-foot climbing ropes were attached to the old bridge, then you tied on, walked along the side of the gorge to the other bridge. You climbed over the rail, the ropes were tightened and then you just jumped off. Rob went first and I thought he was going to hit the bottom. You free fall the first 100 feet then you swing under the old bridge. The guys on the old bridge then lower you off. My go next. I thought I would shout "Geronimo" but as my stomach hit my mouth and nothing came out! Andy went next, but as he jumped the police arrived. It was illegal to jump here as it was a main road and the bridge was between two tunnels. Drivers had come out of a tunnel to see some bloke jump and had panicked. The gay barman could speak fluent Spanish and persuaded the police that, as foreigners, we didn't know it was illegal. One of the pub locals filmed the jumps, so we had a film show at the pub with lots of beer.

Another highlight of Calpe is the Penon d'Ifach, a 1,000-foot monolith sticking out of the sea. It is 800 feet of climbing in eight pitches. On the sixth pitch you climb a long slab and end up on a horizontal ridge a foot wide, where you sit 'a cheval', or 'like a horse'. You can suddenly see 800 feet down to Calpe harbour. It took two-and-a-half hours. About 100 metres away is the top cairn, so we decided to walk to it to have lunch. There is an easy walk down the other side. Coming up were two plump English girls. One shouted to the other, "Get the fags and coke out Trace, I'm ****ing knackered." Just like Sharon and Tracy in Viz!!

Now free of children, Joan and I could travel abroad every year. We did the usual, Greece, Spain, Portugal, France, and Tenerife. Twice, in 1993 and 1998, the school took a group to Languedoc with PGL, an English kids' tour company. They went on a bus which took twenty hours. As extra staff, Joan and I drove across France in three days, stopping at all the sights such as Paris, the Dordogne, Chablis and coming back via Italy or Spain. The holiday was multi water sports. The highlight for me as a canoe instructor was a trip down the river Ardeche. The Ardeche is in a limestone gorge with rapids every half mile.

Taking kids out in the country and introducing them to skiing, climbing, canoeing, sailing, and hill walking was a pleasure. Many of them took one of them up after leaving. I have met many ex-pupils that remember me taking them on trips. Several of them said it had changed their life!

In the 1980s the school (Lindsey) was really successful and had a good staff. We did fun shows for the kids and I wrote a few sketches, like Mastermind where all the answers were "pass". All except one: "What three words are the most common answers for Lindsey school kids?" Of course, the reply was, "I don't know." Correct. I was also the master in charge of staff booze-ups (unofficially). Derek, the a head of year, said, "You like real ale, Pete. Shall we organise a trip?" So we put up a notice saying, "If you like real ale – sign up here." Within two days we noticed two women had signed up. I approached Sarah and was surprised she was a real ale fan. "I'm not," she said. "So why did you sign up?" "It's sexist," she replied. It didn't say men only! "It's still sexist." The list got bigger, with more women, until a big bus was needed. When I posted a list of pick-up places, as many staff lived in outlying villages, the women started moaning that the pick- up places were not to their liking and began to drop out. We had to cancel! Plan B. I then went round secretly asking 'the boys' if they wanted to go on our 'field trip' at the end of term. We got the school minibus driver to take twelve blokes to a real ale pub in the country. We all put £10 in the kitty and drank until closing time. We did this for years and the women never asked to go. Success! They did start to moan at me a bit, because their husbands were not very well the following morning!

Joan and I had a friend who had moved to Norway and married a Norwegian. She had been there for some years and none of her friends or relatives had been to see them. So, in 1992 we caught the ferry from Newcastle to Bergan. We took Ann-Marie as well. Our route took us through the fiords, over the longest fiord, passing the deepest fiord, the highest cliff (Troll Wall) and the highest waterfall. Our friend, Dawn, lived on an island not far from Trondheim. The island is called Froya. To get to it we had to cross another island called Hitra. The journey needed five ferries to get us there. Norway is expensive, so we took a lot of food and drink and stopped at campsites which all had huts with electricity, water, a fridge, crockery, and cutlery. All for £20 a night. We did find a pub: I had a pint and the girls half a pint. It cost £12!! Froya had one road, which went around it. The centre of the island is moorland and lakes just like Rannoch moor in Scotland. This isn't surprising as Scotland and Norway are made of the same rocks as they were once the same mountain range before plate tectonics split them up. They also have the same weather – wet! The island depends on fishing. Dawn's husband, Edgar, took me fishing in the fiord and after two hours caught a barrel of cod and haddock. All without any bait, just lures. I also cycled round the island and climbed all the rocks I could find.

In 1999 we decided to return to Norway, but by way of Denmark and Sweden. In the queue for the ferry was Sandi Toksvig, who had also been in the queue the last time we went to Norway. I met her on a stairway and asked if she was following me. She is tiny! It's difficult to see how big or little people are on TV. We drove across Denmark to Copenhagen, which is a beautiful city, clean, and full of interesting buildings and history. Then onto Sweden via Lake Vattern, which is Sweden's second largest lake at ninety miles long and fifteen miles wide! Walking down to the lake we passed wild cherry trees, raspberries, and strawberries, so we had a free fruit salad. We stayed at campsites again and stayed in the well-equipped huts. Then up to Stockholm, along to the Baltic coast and Gulf of Bothnia, to Sundsvall and Umea. The Umea campsite had 100 huts which were all full, so we had to stay in a wooden tent, which had no electricity or water. But it was cheap. We even swam in lakes and the sea at sixty degrees north. Turning inland we crossed the Arctic circle near Jokkmokk, the Sammi capital of the Lapps, still in shorts. Over the mountains to Kiruna, where they mine haematite ore, and into Norway, at Narvik, sixty one degrees north. Now south to Trondheim via the village of Hell! and onto Froya. I expected a ferry to the island, but in seven years they had cut two tunnels to cut out the ferries. The Norwegians are tunnel mad! Even in August it never got really dark. At midnight it was like a sunset. Sea eagles are common here and one took our friend's cat.

Summer camp

Me and Joan with the grandchildren

Climbing with pot on leg Climbing in the Med   Bridge jump

Penon down to harbour   Canoeing in the Ardeche

Chapter 6.

2000s: Retirement and big mountains worldwide.

I began thinking of early retirement as the school was rapidly going downhill due to a dreadful new headmaster. My geography department had had the best 'A'-level results in the school at one point, but we were now losing our sixth form. I could go at fifty-five with a slight loss of pension, but I thought of my sanity above money, so I intended to go at fifty-five, in October 2001. In the summer of that year Joan and I flew to San Francisco where we stayed for three days. On arrival at the hotel, the doorman heard our accent and asked if we knew the Queen. I said, "No, but my mother has met her." That impressed him. We hired a car and drove over the Golden Gate Bridge to Sacramento and Lake Tahoe. I was impressed with the wildlife, which was almost tame. Eagles, chipmunks, and blue jays were everywhere. The blue jays would fly onto your table, snatch a sachet of sugar, and fly off. Yosemite next. A stunning place where El Capitan dominates. A granite monolith half a mile high. A climber's paradise, but too hot in summer. After that, King's Canyon and Sequoia national park. All fantastic in their own way. We saw a rattle snake and tarantula on the same day.

The Americans were very polite and when we spoke, they usually said, "You guys from Australia?" They also eat too much. Every meal was massive. We ate breakfast at cafes and just wanted a coffee and toast. The nearest to toast was a stack of cakes, large or small. We asked for a small stack between us. "Not a stack each?" It was thick pancakes with maple syrup. All the American customers were having steak and eggs! Pubs were rare in California, but we did find one which said 'Pub' above the door. It was like the Wild West, with a fat barmaid who slid your pint of beer down the bar to you! It was the first country we had visited which was English speaking but several times we met Mexicans who never spoke English! Two weeks after returning it was 9/11 in New York!

I decided to work until Christmas instead of retiring on my October birthday. I was counting the days down. What a relief to get out of teaching, which had become a nightmare. Retirement at last!

Retirement – and a new life and decade. I had made it. The first day back at school after Christmas was fantastic. I could stay in bed. However, Joan was still working, so I was now a house husband. I had to learn how the washing machine worked, how to iron and do all the housewifey things. I did all the jobs by ten o'clock, so the rest of my day was mine. When Joan got home, there was a cup of coffee waiting and tea was cooked and ready. I didn't have to learn to cook, as I ould always cook and bake. Home-made bread from the Aga is brilliant. Within a week I had a phone call from Graham, who was a builder. "Can you come out of retirement and help me and operate the cement mixer, as I've got a wall to build?" So, for the next few years I became an occasional labourer. I also had time to try other adventure sports like gliding, paragliding, parachuting, potholing, and sub-aqua diving. Paragliding is easy to learn and would buy one if I lived in a hilly area. Potholing is for masochists! Diving is okay if you live in the Med. But too cold in the UK.

Art. I had an 'A'-level in art, but had never used water colours, so I joined an adult group to learn. All the group, except me, were older women, mostly called Mavis. The teacher went very slowly, but after lesson three he taught how to do washes. So I went home and painted a few things which contained washes. My favourite was a dragon's head, which was very good, but I had added a simple colour wash around the edge of the paper. The tutor never mentioned the dragon, but said my wash was good. After a term I gave up with the teacher and bought some books. "How to paint water colours." One day when Joan came back from work, I had painted four landscapes in a day. After six months I had enough paintings to hold an art exhibition. I also framed a dozen of my Grandad's ink drawings of the unknown women to show. I had painted landscapes, birds, flowers, portraits, churches, and animals, but the landscapes sold best. I decided to have another exhibition, with copies of my Grandad's women, Joan's handbags, Ann-Marie's jewellery and some of my sister's paintings.

As I have 7,000 slides, mostly of mountain scenes, I had the best ones enlarged and printed. In my next exhibition I added these to my paintings. The photographs sold like hot cakes. In both my exhibitions I sold about £1,000 worth!

With all the free time I had, I began to cycle more. My friend Pete, from the youth hostel, had now retired to Spain. I planned to go and see him and started to go to Spanish lessons. After two terms, and in the first summer of retirement, I flew to Torrevieja with my bike in a bike box and cycled in the sun for two weeks. I had cycled across France as a youth, so I might cycle across Spain the next year. The problem is when to go. It's too hot in summer and as the interior of Spain is 1,000 metres high, and it's too cold in winter. So, in 2002, Joan drove me to Portsmouth, where I caught the ferry to Bilbao. My journey was planned, but I hadn't booked accommodation as it was off-season. The map said that I needed a small road out of the port and across the river. I was first off the ferry and the police stopped me to look at my passport. I followed the 'salida' signs and the police said nothing. I ended up on the motorway! It was rush hour. Eight o'clock. I got off at the first exit and ended up in the town centre. Bilbao is in the Basque region and the language is nothing like Spanish. Fortunately, they all spoke Spanish as well. I found my way out of town and headed for the Rioja region. Within two hours I was on a pass at 2,000 feet. The minor road I was on went through a gorge, along with the motorway and the railway. Very tight and complicated. I arrived at Haro, in the Rioja country, and stayed in a basic bed and breakfast.

The next day I was heading for Soria, but not on the main road. I got lost in Najera and asked a lorry driver the way. I only understood two words. 'Semaforos' and 'a la derecha'. At the traffic lights, turn right. My basic Spanish worked and I got good at asking directions. This minor road took me up a valley and over the Sierra Demanda. As I turned a corner, I heard machinery, which surprised me as there was nothing on the road. It was a lorry and JCB scaping a mud slide off the road, which I had to walk through. Leaving the valley, the road steepened and rose to 4000 feet. Then down to Salina de los Infantes. I had trouble finding a place to stay, as the first two places obviously didn't want a sweaty cyclist. However, the biggest hotel let me in. I was the only one staying there. Dinner didn't start until half past nine, which is normal in Spain. They all eat late.

Day three was a short trip to Soria, over another 4000-foot pass. I decided to stay for two nights and have a rest day as I was a little saddle sore. I hadn't cycle toured for forty years and needed a rest. The problem was that I hadn't changed or washed my shorts and top, as they were always dry when I reached the towns. However, they had dried up salty sweat which caused the soreness. From then on, I always washed my top and shorts in the shower and dried them by hanging them out of the window.

Day four was a rest day. Sunbathed in park. Cold in the morning as we were 3,000 feet up.

Day five. A long day: 120 kilometres, but mostly downhill. A lonely road. I saw no cars, people, farmers, and few villages. At Cetina, a small village, there was a sharp dip across the road, which was a drain. I heard a "ping" from my back wheel. I stopped an hour later for lunch. As I moved my bike, I noticed the wheel was catching on the brake. That ping had been a spoke snapping! I tried to remove it, but failed, so I taped it to another spoke. A few miles down the road I realised I had a puncture. I stopped to change the inner tube, when a lorry approached. I thumbed a lift to the next town, where I thought there might be a bike shop. The driver spoke no English. He wasn't going to the town I was aiming for, but a small town which had spa water. His lorry was collecting water bottles. I asked if the town had a bike shop. He laughed and said it had no shops at all! When he arrived, I checked my wheel and found that I had turned the broken spoke the wrong way and it had punctured the inner tube. I reset the spoke and set off up a small pass with my wheel wobbling and the back brake released. I was dreading going downhill. Fortunately, there was no more downhill and I arrived at Molina de Aragon. I found a hotel and asked if they had a bike shop. She said they did, but it didn't open until five o'clock. It was like someone's front room, but he replace my spoke, straightened my wheel, and told me off for riding a bike with panniers on a racing wheel.

Day six, was in the Sierra Cuenca, a limestone plateau at 5,000 feet. I was chased out of town by four Alsatian dogs which were loose in a field! There were some steep, long hills here, but I had a low gear and managed okay. I arrived at Tragacete, which was a small mountain village with lots of hotels. In the hotel I chose, I was the only resident. He let me off twenty per cent. This village is at the same hight as Ben Nevis! Although high, it was hot.

It was nearly all downhill to the town of Cuenca. The biggest town I was to stay at. I chose a hotel on the main street, which was busy, so I asked a bloke at a news stall to watch my bike as I went in. I booked in and asked, "What about my bike?" "El ascensor," he said. I had to put my bike upright to get it in the lift! Cuenca is a beautiful little town with 'casas colgadas', or hanging houses. It was quite a posh hotel and had a good restaurant, so I had trout.

Day seven was cloudy and dull. It was going to be a long day, so I cut it in half. Up to 4,000 feet again and almost in cloud. I stayed in a boring town called Motilla. Nothing to do or see.

Day eight was cloudy again but with thunderstorms. The roads were wet, but the showers narrowly missed me. Then the road stopped. They were resurfacing and had stripped the road back to rock! There was mud everywhere and I had to walk for two miles. I was heading for Alcala de Jucar, which is in a spectacular gorge nearly 1,000 feet deep. Fantastic zigzags to the village. I stopped at a small bar/hotel and went in to find the usual group of old blokes drinking and smoking. As I went in they all stopped speaking and stared at me like I was an alien. I was covered in mud from the waist down. I asked the barman if he had a room. He said nothing, and just slapped a key on the bar and said, "secunda planta" – second floor. The river Jucar had made an incised meander, which was so thin that they had cut tunnels from one side to the other. Spectacular! I had a meal in another bar while the blokes watched the bullfight on TV. It's as popular as football!

Day nine, I woke up to fog. My stay at the little hotel cost twenty Euros for bed and breakfast! As I climbed up the winding hill out of the other side of the gorge, it started to get lighter until I broke out into bright sunlight. I was now far south and the rest of the journey was in hot sunshine. A long easy day in the sun to Yecla. The manager of the hotel there noticed I was cycling and said that there was a wedding party that night at the hotel and it would be noisy. I said that I'll sleep okay. So, he put me on the top floor, out of the way.

Day ten – the last day, but still at 2,000 feet. Only twenty miles from the coast did I come to a big downhill section to sea level. I stayed at Pete's place for two weeks cycling and decided to catch a train back to Bilbao. It was an overnight train. At seven o'clock the conductor woke me up and babbled something at me in unintelligible Spanish. I realised, when we arrived, he was telling me the train was an hour late. I now had less than two hours to get to the ferry, fourteen kms away. I could not find the ordinary road and asked several people, who all directed me to the motorway. Time was running out so I went on the motorway. Three kilometres to go and a policeman ran across the road shouting at me. I carried on, until a police car pulled me over. I explained in my poor Spanish, that there were no signs for other roads in Bilbao, that the train was late, and that my ferry left in thirty minutes and the next one was in three days. He told me to ride on the hard shoulder (which I was doing) and they would follow me with their hazards on. The last bit to the port was downhill as I left the motorway and I was exceeding the speed limit of fifty kilometres per hour. As I entered the port I expected to be stopped and fined. But they had gone! I went to the head of the queue and boarded, just in time. The ferry left an hour late! I had a couple of beers and went for a swim in the pool. We spotted over 1,000 dolphins and many whales in the Bay of Biscay, which is apparently famous for cetaceans.

For the next ten years I flew out to Torrevieja to stay with Pete and cycle in the sun. The area around Torrevieja is rural, where fruit and veg are grown. At certain roundabouts I noticed young ladies in skimpy clothing, sitting on chairs with a parasol. I asked Pete what they were going there. He said they were Russian prostitutes. Another English friend asked how much they charged. I said that I only took two Euros with me. He replied that I would get some change! I didn't participate, but they always said "Hola" as I passed.

Mountaineering worldwide. This had been the first of my expeditions in the 'noughties'. The climbing club kept on climbing in the winter abroad and tried Corsica, Croatia, and Sardinia. All fantastic venues. Each May I cycled in Spain, based in Torrevieja. I tried to tour on my bike to Granada and the Sierra Nevada, but west of Lorca, after Velez Rubio, the only road to Granada was a motorway. There is no other road! So I had to double-back to the coast and head back. Even then I had to go on a bit of motorway, but this time the cops didn't see me! The next year I hired a car and put my bike in the back and drove to Granada, where I cycled up the Sierra Nevada to the ski resort of Solynieve at over 8,000 feet. A twenty-mile hill! Where the road stops, there is a track up to Pico de Veleta at over 10,000 feet. An easy walk, but an ice axe is necessary, even in May. I cycled this route three more times in the following years.

2007 - a big year: Aconcagua, Argentina in February, Tenerife in April, Spain in May, Norway in August. From now on I thought it was time to see the world, before I got too old. Aconcagua was the first of my seven trips to South and Central America.

Aconcagua is the highest mountain outside the Himalaya and the highest in the Americas at 6,960 metres. It was a twenty-nine-hour journey via Manchester, Madrid, Santiago and a twenty-five-minute flight over the Andes to Mendoza. Mendoza is a beautiful city, full of trees, parks and lovely women! My guide was called Ryan, an American from Atlanta. The only other client was Graham, who was English, but lived in California. After a couple of days, we drove to Penitentes, a ski station on top of an 8,000-foot pass to Chile. Next day we began walking up the Rio de Vacas, or cow river. After two days walking up the same valley, we eventually glimpsed Aconcagua. Our gear was carried by mules, which ferried us across the shallow river. One more day's walk and we arrived at base camp, Plaza Argentina at 4,200 metres. First stop was to see the doctor, who took our blood pressure, pulse, and oxygen intake. Mine were all fine. In fact, my heart rate was lower than Ryan's. Graham's blood pressure was too high and the doctor gave him some pills. Next day he went to the doctor again to find his blood pressure still too high. He got an injection. Ryan and I went up to camp one as a warm up, but the doctor wouldn't let Graham go. We got to the camp in two hours. Ryan was astonished that a sixty-one-year-old had done it that fast, as it usually took most five hours!

Graham's blood pressure remained high and he was sent back home! The next night I was so snug in my sleeping bag, I was sleeping naked, when suddenly my tent hit me in the face and woke me up. People were running about outside in headtorches and shouting. There was a gale blowing and some tents were down. Ryan came to my tent and asked if I was okay. I said yes and he tightened my guy ropes up. I stayed in bed. Next morning the campsite was covered in snow, which the locals said was unusual in February. A helicopter arrived and took four people away with frost bite, as they had been caught out on the mountain. Ryan and I took a load of gear up to camp one. He gave me lots of food, cooking gear, and a big shovel. My rucksack was so heavy I had to put it on a big rock and put my arms through the straps as I couldn't lift it off the floor! No water up here, even though we were walking up a glacier, which was covered in rock. We snapped a bit of penitentes off to melt for cooking. These are strange blades of ice sticking up through the glacial rubble, caused by wind and sun. There were thousands of them. We were both given a large, black plastic bag in which to deposit your faeces, as it was illegal to "do it" outdoors. If you were away for a few days and your bag was empty, you would be fined! Trying to "do it" in a plastic bag in a gale is extremely difficult, to say the least. The next day it was blowing a gale again, which is quite common in this region. We could hardly stand up. I asked Ryan how long it would last and he asked base camp and he was told three days. I said I'm not spending three days up here in a tent, so we went back down to base camp. We were now running out of time, as I had a plane to catch in four days, so we reluctantly decided to go back. Back in Mendoza I tried to get an earlier flight. No luck. I had three days to kill. Ryan went back home and I stayed in Mendoza. I organised a paragliding session, a mountain bike ride, rafting, and a wine tour. A bus came to my hotel each time to pick me up. On the wine tour, I was first pick-up, then an old couple, and then an attractive young blond, who, on an empty bus, sat next to me! I said that she didn't look Argentinian and she replied, in an American accent, "I'm Swiss". "Why the American accent?," I asked. "It's Canadian actually. I was brought up in Canada." She could speak English, German, French, and Spanish.

They have many vineyards in Mendoza. I visited a wine tasting shop and they said they would fly me a case back. So, I chose six bottles and paid for the freight. The case arrived a week after I returned. The delivery driver said, "What you got in there, mate? Drugs?" I said, "No, why?" He said that he had had it for a week and they wouldn't let him deliver it. Two days later I get an e-mail from customs asking for my VAT details. I replied to say I am not an importer, just a tourist. I then get a bill for forty Pounds wine tax. I ring the office and was told about import taxes etc. I replied that, with the freight charges and taxes, each bottle would cost me eight pounds and I can buy Argentinian wine from Asda for three pounds. I am NOT paying! I get a reply saying that due to the excessive paperwork they will drop the case!

In April the club spent a week in Tenerife rock climbing and in May I spent a month in Spain cycling in the Alpujarras and around Torrevieja. The Alpujarra valley, south of the Sierra Nevada range, is fantastic countryside with beautiful white villages hanging on the valley sides. Trevelez village is at 1,470 metres altitude and is a centre for producing Jamon Serrano.

Norway. Our third trip to Norway. Joan wanted to see a moose as there are moose signs everywhere on the roads – because if you hit one, they are so big, the one-tonne body crushes the car and driver! We were told that if we drove north of Trondheim there was a park that had moose(s?) called Namsskogan. It was a huge park with moose, deer, bears, otters, and many birds. At feeding time, we saw the moose at close quarters so that Joan could stroke them. We returned to our friend's house on Froya, where Edgar had now got lots of crab pots in the fiord. We caught dozens and feasted on white claw meat. The next we were fed moose steak, which Joan surprisingly ate! On the way back we stayed at the famous Geiranger fiord, which is famous for cruise trips, even though it is miles inland. After this trip they stopped the Newcastle – Bergan ferry, which meant a much longer trip to Norway.

My trip to Argentina encouraged me to travel to worldwide in the following years, travelling abroad up to six times a year. Lots of mountains and volcanoes to climb in the next twelve years.

2008 saw me visit Mexico, Kalymnos, Ireland and Nepal. A good year. I had a short trip up Mexico's highest peak, Orizaba or Citlaltepetl, in Aztec, at 5,700 metres, or 18,865 feet. Mexico City is huge, with a population of over twenty million at 7,000 feet. We drove through Puebla to a small village called Tlachachuca, at 9,000 feet. We stayed in an old soap factory, used as a climbing refuge and owned by the local surgeon. Next day we were driven in two old American Dodge trucks for a three-hour, bumpy, off-road journey to a hut at 13,900 feet. The hut had no water, no electricity, no fuel, no toilets and was single-glazed. It had Alpine accommodation, which means three long wooden bunks for all of us. Next day we walked with all the camping gear to 15,000 feet and made camp. Clouds came rolling in from the coast each afternoon, but never reached our altitude. Before we ate there was a huge roar as a rock avalanche came down only a hundred metres from us! This mountain is a dormant volcano and the rock is very unstable. It last erupted 500 years ago.

Up at one a.m. and we climbed in the dark with head torches, but the moon was full and you could see okay in the snow. At the base of the cone we put on our crampons, roped up in fours, and set off up a thirty-five degree slope for three boring hours! We reached the top at sunrise. The crater is still warm and smelling of sulphur. The shadow of the cone stretched to the horizon – a fantastic sight. On the way back to Mexico City we saw Popocatepetl erupting. We had a day to kill before going home, so we visited Teotihuacan, which had two pyramids higher than Giza's. The town around them is thought to have had 30,000 inhabitants.

Kalymnos in May was a great week as usual. Four of us climbed Trela, which means 'madness' in Greek. It was in a huge cave packed with stalactites, which we climbed around. It overhangs by twelve metres. Four days after returning from Greece I was off to Spain for a month's cycling. I did 1,766 kilometres, including Solynieve at 8,500 feet.

Joan and I decided to tour Ireland in August. Holyhead to Dublin on the ferry. We stayed in a B&B on the coast and took a bus into Dublin. It rained all day! We then drove to Galway, which is beautiful, but busy. It rained. We drove to the Burren and the cliffs of Mohar and it was sunny! Next day to Killarney as I wanted to climb Carrauntoohil, Ireland's highest mountain, but as the cloud level was

100 feet and it was raining, I didn't bother. Ireland is a wonderful place and the people are lovely. But the weather is crap!

To complete my year, I went to Nepal to try Ama Dablam, a 23,000-foot mountain shaped like the Matterhorn. It was a month's trip with a big team of Americans, Greeks, a Swiss, German, Czech, Slovenian, and a Dutchman. I was the only Brit. Flight to Doha. It was thirty degrees centigrade at midnight! Landed at Kathmandu. Picked up and taken to a hotel by car. Driving is suicidal. I had no idea which side of the road they drove on, as they were on the right, left, centre, and on the pavement. We met the others and went to buy any gear that we didn't have. All made in little sweat shops in the old town. Narrow, crowded streets, with scooters, cows, and rickshaws. We stood out like sore thumbs in western gear. Beggars everywhere. I went to an ATM to get some Nepalese Rupees. A hundred Pounds' worth gave me thousands of Rupees. Outside were three or four beggars, as they knew we had lots of money. On day three we went to the airport which was total chaos. We were loaded onto small single engine aircraft. I was sitting near the front and could almost touch the pilot. We flew between the peaks and when we turned to land at Lukla, we turned to fly into the valley side. A Greek climber said, "You can see a little landing strip half way up the slope." It was about 150 metres long and ended at a vertical face. We learned later that there had been many fatal crashes here, when mist had descended as the plane approached and had hit the cliff below!

First day was an easy one as we were already at 9,000 feet. The path is the Everest trail along the Dudh Cosi valley. We crossed many bouncy wire bridges which were okay as long as you didn't have to share them with a yak. They were common, as they carried most of our equipment. There are dozens of places to stay on the trail. All basic but clean and cheap. Next day was to Namche Bazaar, where we stayed for two days to acclimatise at 11,000 feet. We walked up a hill to see Everest for the first time. Next day to Pangboche, where we saw our objective – Ama Dablam. A beautiful pyramidal peak. Pangboche had a Buddist temple, a bakery, and centre for e-mailing and phoning home. The local Lama blessed us all and gave us a sacred string to hang round our necks, in exchange for a few Rupees. We left the path the next day to go up to Ama Dablam Base Camp. There were several groups from all over the world here, including some New Zealanders, whom I had met earlier that year in Mexico!

The campsite was huge, flat, and with grass, which is unusual for this region. We could even have a shower if we asked the cooks to fill a pump spray with hot water and then went to the shower tent. We were woken each morning by two cooks asking if we wanted tea or coffee in bed. Then a big breakfast. A group of us went to Advanced Base Camp to put up a few tents, as a first day of acclimatisation.

Next day was a rest day when we could wash some clothes. It was also my sixty-second birthday and the cooks baked me a cake and they all sang happy birthday to me! More acclimatisation the day after when we went up to Advanced Base to sleep. The evening was fantastic above the clouds that covered Base Camp each afternoon. The Milky Way, Venus, and millions of stars shining so brightly, as there is zero light pollution here. The next morning, we went up to Camp One at the beginning of the ridge and back down to Base Camp. A long day.

We were told we could have a rest day and descend to the main path and Tenboche to stay in a lodge with a fire and have a warm night. We met lots of groups from home and Australia. We even met an Uzbekistan girl called Xixingma, who spoke excellent English. She worked in the financial sector in London.

Back up to Base Camp the next day and now acclimatised, so up to Camp Two on the narrow ridge. Fixed ropes protect you from the steep drop as you go horizontally, but there are two sections of slab climbing where you have to use jumars to stop you from falling. The second slab was about twenty-five metres high at about VS grade. Easy at sea level, but at 18,000 feet you got out of breath when you did a move like a mantelshelf. I was also wearing bendy walking boots! We got to Camp Two and left some gear and abseiled down. That night at Base Camp I was awoken by a big rumble, I thought that it was strange to hear thunder as the night was clear with no clouds. A minute later my tent shook! In the morning Dan Mazur came to camp after he had climbed Cho Oyu. He was the owner of the mountaineering company and famous for rescuing a climber on Everest. The rumble in the night had been a huge serac collapse on Ama Dablam above the ridge. In the next few days there were three more collapses, which fell on the route. There were 300 people from all over the world here to climb Ama Dablam, but it was too dangerous. Most of the Greeks went back, but a few of us went back up to Camp Two to retrieve our stashed gear.

The rest of us descended to Panboche and stayed in a lodge. A pot-bellied stove in the middle of the room was filled with fuel – dried yak dung! The woman filling it just wiped her hands on her apron and went back to the kitchen to cook our meal. Did she wash her hands?

Namche Bazaar next. Jason, the group leader, Kyle, and me found a pub which sold whisky. It said Scotch whisky on the bottle, but was made in Nepal. Jason met some friends who invited us to their lodge after dinner, so we went and found them playing a drinking game. We joined in and got drunk on chang and whisky. Kyle disappeared, so we went looking for him. Back at the lodge we found him in a bedroom flat out, with a bucket next to his bed. How he found his way back, nobody knows. He had a mega hangover the next day. We strolled down to Lukla to fly back to Kathmandu and booked in at a better hotel with a pool. We had three days to kill, so a few of us went on a trip to the jungle: Jason, Kyle, Tony, Kori, and Brent, the Americans, Penelope the Greek lady, and Michael the Slovenian. A six-hour journey downhill to the jungle, where we had an elephant ride and a trip down the river in a dug-out canoe. We saw rhino, crocodile, and dozens of birds and butterflies. Back to Kathmandu for a last meal together and home via Doha.

2009: No big mountains this year, just rock climbing in Mallorca, cycling in Spain, and touring in Scotland. Mallorca was wet! We did have an eventful day when climbing near the sea. It rained, so a few of us went for a swim, including Ollie. He was pink when he came out and everyone else was white with cold. As Ollie was drying out, he collapsed. John was called over to see him, as he is a doctor. Ollie was hypothermic! We revived him, covered him up, and gave him a hot drink. Luckily, he recovered as we were two miles from the road.

Spain – cycling. As well as cycling, I packed some walking gear, including an ice axe, and went up to Solynieve in the car and walked up to Pico Veleta, which is the second highest peak in the Sierra Nevada. They were still skiing here in May! Later on, I met John, the climbing doctor, and we traversed the Bernia Ridge. This ridge can only be traversed by climbers, as there are two abseils and a rock climb on it.

North west Scotland. I hadn't been north of Skye, so Joan and I went on a B&B trip to the north west Highlands. We went for eleven days and it rained for ten! At the Kyle of Lochalche and Skye, it was sunny. At Ullapool, I left Joan in town so I could go up Stac Pollaidh. It rained, so I came back. Next day we went further north and as we passed Stac Pollaidh, I could see the top. We veered off and I put on my running shoes and said to Joan that would only be ninety minutes. I ran up and down it in sixty-five minutes, just in time to meet Joan, who had driven to the coast whilst I'd been running. Just in time as it then rained all day. Up to Lochinver to do Suilven, but guess what? It rained. So we went home.

Me with fish in Norway

Arctic circle, near Jokkmokk

Yosemite

Puffin

Arrival at Torrevieja

Top of Sierra Nevada

Aconcagua

Me with Penitentes

Orizaba crater

Shadow of Orizaba

Ama Dablam

Climbing Ama Dablam

Chapter 7.

2010s: Worldwide travel, mountains, and a becoming a pensioner.

The Teenies. 2010. Mountaineering and climbing in forty-plus countries, as well as becoming a carer and great-grandad. I now have a state pension as well as a school pension, so I can travel even more!

I started being a carer for my Uncle Ron, the RAF hero. His wife had died in 2004 and they had no children, so he was lost. I began taking my mother over to see him every few months and taking them out for a meal. We brought him over for Christmas each year, but he steadily got worse and had carers looking after him. He began to give up and stay in bed, so I decided to bring him over to Cleethorpes permanently. He stayed with Mother, but it soon became apparent that she could not cope, so he went into a home, where he lasted a year and died peacefully in his sleep. I organised an RAF funeral for him, with the local RAF group bearing a flag and a representative from 617 Squadron attending. His coffin came in with the Dam Busters theme. It was a fitting send off for a great bloke!

The climbing club went to Turkey for the first time. Inland from Antalya there was a new climbing venue. The accommodation was basic, to say the least. Garden sheds with a couple of beds in. No furniture, chairs, or anything but a couple of nails in the wall to hang a coat. The nearest village was a mile away and had one basic shop that sold local vegetables. Nearest town was ten miles away. Nearest restaurant half a mile away, so we tried that. Up an open stairwell with no rails and a bare venue with a few tables and chairs and bare walls. We asked for a menu to be told, "Chicken or fish."

We asked for drinks and it was, "Coke or Fanta." The only heating was a pot-bellied stove in the middle of the floor with the pipe snaking to the window which was dangling from a electrical wire from the ceiling. The wire was attached to the only lightbulb in the room! Health and safety has not reached here yet! We did find a better venue for eating, but this was two miles down the hill. However, we did find a German lady that cooked Turkish cuisine at her large house and she picked us up in her van! Despite the basic conditions, the rock climbing was fantastic.

Joan and I went on a package holiday to Gran Canaria, which was okay if you chose the right resort.

I had started cycling with a group of old cyclists like myself. Every Wednesday we would cycle sixty miles in the Lincolnshire Wolds. Four of us went over to France in two camper vans in September to climb Mont Ventoux, which is infamous in the Tour de France. As a warm-up on the first day we did 100 kilometres circumnavigating the Ventoux. There are three ways to the top. The hardest route is from Bedoin, which is twenty kilometres long and has an eight-kilometre stretch of ten per cent. Six kilometres from the top is a welcome café and one kilometre from the top is Tommy Simpson's memorial where he fell off his bike and later died in hospital. The last six kilometres are within a desert of white limestone and there is no shelter. It was thirty degrees centigrade in the shade and there wasn't any. Descending to Malaucene I touched eighty kilometres-per-hour and overtook every car and cyclist!

2011: Five trips this year, including some big mountains. Ecuador. This would be the first time I had set foot on the equator so before I set off I had my photo taken on the Greenwich meridian at Cleethorpes. Zero degrees longitude and then zero degrees latitude.

Manchester, Heathrow, Miami, and Quito. Twenty hours travelling. Arrived at midnight and met the only other mountaineer, Fiella, a French Algerian. She was too serious and didn't seem to have a sense of humour, so I tested her by noticing she was wearing flip-flops and said, "Did you know flip-flops were invented by a Frenchman – Philippe Feloppe?" Not a titter! We chilled for two days acclimatising as Quito is 9,000 feet up. We met our guide Rodrigez who took us to Mitad del Mundo or the equator, a tourist park which is not quite on the equator. So we went to the proper equator where you can test the Coriolis force by the water experiment either side of the zero degees line. Impressive.

In the next few days we climbed several volcanoes, each higher than the last: Cuichoca, Fuya-Fuya, Imbabura, Illinizas, and Cayambe. Before we climbed Illinizas, we stayed at a lodge with a group of Germans who had lost their leader the day before as he fell 200 metres to his death! We stayed at the Cayambe refuge at 4,600 metres and went up it at night. This volcano is right on the equator. It had a big glacier on it. Ecuador is the only place on the planet with permanent ice at the equator. Cotopaxi next. This is one of the highest active volcanoes on Earth. We drove up to the refuge at 4,867 metres in a Toyota four-wheel drive. Off at one a.m. and walked uphill for five hours in the dark. The sky at night at this height is amazing. The Milky way is ablaze with stars and Venus looked like a small moon. We reached the top ninety minutes after sunrise. We were 4,867 metres high and two miles above the clouds! It erupted only thirty years before and was still smoking. It has a huge double crater with huge snow banks around it.

On our last day we became tourists and visited Quilotoa lagoon, a two-kilometre-wide crater filled with water. There were Ecuadorian ladies there dressed in traditional bowler hats, colourful shawls, and long skirts. The ethnic population are all small, so I asked Rodrigez if they would mind if I had my photo taken with them. They said okay but asked for a dollar each. They made me feel tall!

Kalymnos as usual in May. Always good – climbing, food, drink, and company. Forty-four routes. The club tried Lundy for a week's climbing. Lund is Norse for a Puffin and y means an island. A small granite island in the Bristol channel, facing the Atlantic gales. The boat takes ninety minutes from Ilfracombe and it is usually rough. It was, and many people were sick. Steve and I went to the bar for a beer. The island is flat and the climbs are all sea cliffs. We camped in the foul weather and were saved by the excellent pub each evening. One day it so windy we couldn't climb, so we walked around the island in three hours. There are some classic climbs here like the Devil's Slide and Double Diamond which is an arched sea stack.

Joan and I returned to Norway as our English friend, Dawn, had died suddenly earlier that year. The Newcastle to Bergan ferry had now stopped, so we had to take the Harwich to Esbjerg ferry, then drive up the length of Denmark to Aalborg and then the ferry from Hirtshals to Kristiansand. Then two more days driving through Norway to Froya. On the way out of a town I was stopped by the police for speeding. It was the first time I had seen a policeman in Norway. I always drove slowly in Norway as the limits are low, but as I drove out of this town, I was in the country which had an eighty-kilometres-per-hour limit. I was doing sixty-six kilometres per hour in a sixty limit. I explained I was a tourist and thought I was out of town. He said the sixty kilometres sign was fifty metres up the road. I thought he would let me off, but no. The fine was 300 Euros! On Froya, we met Edgar's new woman, Margareet, and the next day I started off to walk across the island, but the markers ran out and I got lost. There is no decent map and all the land is the same – low heather hills and lots of lakes. Four days to drive back! Next time, I think we'll fly.

2012 A quiet year for me, a sun holiday in Cyprus and then two trips to Provence, one cycling and one climbing. The winter in England had been so wet that I decided to get some early sun, so I booked a quick trip to Cyprus. Very sunny even in April. It seems to be full of Russians. There was even a Russian karaoke bar! In May we tried climbing in Provence for a change. Les Dentelles are fangs of limestone sticking up like teeth. There are so many crags here that we climbed at a different venue every day. In September I was in Provence again, but this time cycling. We stayed at Bourg d'Oisans which is next to famous Alp d'Huez, which is fourteen kilometres long and has twenty-one lacets or bends. The record is thirty-eight minutes, but I pottered up in one hour and twelve minutes. It's not that steep or hard, just long. The seven-kilometre hill up to the village of Oulles was much harder. This village has a population of nineteen and it is a dead end. A long way to the shops. We cycled up a big route every day and did 300 kilometres. On the last day we went up the Col de Lauteret and then up to the Galibier, another famous Tour de France climb. My second time up here, as I had done it in 1965 as an eighteen-year-old. It is 2,642 metres high and quite steep.

2013: A busy year. Six trips and an operation for me. We went to Orgon in Provence for a climbing week with the club. Good limestone as usual, but the weather was a bit showery, as it was only March. On one rainy day we went to see Le Fontaine de Vaucluse – which is a spectacular spring pouring thousands of gallons per minute from a big cave.

At about this time I discovered a lump in my groin, so I visited the doctor. She said it could be just a cyst and sent me for a scan. They said the same and said if it grows or hurts, come back. For a while it was no problem.

In May I took my bike to Normandy via the Newhaven ferry and stayed at a bed and breakfast run by John, who used to teach French at my school, and his wife. I thought May would be nice, but it rained a lot. Mind you, the chalk hills and scenery is quite beautiful. In one forest between the valleys, I found a World War Two Doodlebug on its ramp. It was one of thousands in the area and was preserved and rebuilt after the resistance had blown it up. I arrived back home on Saturday, but had to go to bed early as I was going to Madrid on Sunday.

I went to Madrid with my Spanish group. The idea was to improve our Spanish, but it ends up as a drink and eat fest! As we landed the pilot warned us that it might be bumpy as there were thunderstorms nearby. Just as we were landing the plane wing was struck by lightning on my side. Flash! Bang! We had a guided tour the next day and then visited the Prado. It was my first visit to Madrid and I was impressed with everything. Next day we caught a train to Segovia, a Roman town with a castle and an impressive aqueduct. It is fourteen kilometres long and has a gradient of one in 1,000. How did the Romans do it? After dinner we found a bar only 200 metres from the hotel, so we went for a few beers. After a couple, I suggested Spanish brandy. We all ended up drinking it and had drained a bottle by one a.m. The barman thought we would never leave!

In June I flew to Sofia, Bulgaria, to join Pat, a climbing friend who was living there. Pat drove us to Veliko, the old capital, which had a castle on an incised meander just like Durham. We stopped at a campsite next to a river full of croaking frogs, golden orioles, and kingfishers. The limestone crag was weird with vertical cracks, but no horizontal ones. Going through we saw a pine martin and dozens of strange fungi. The climbing was good, but it was thirty degrees centigrade in the shade. Back in Sofia the nightlife is really good with lots of live music. Pat and I found a large indoor climbing wall which was a bit cooler than outside!

Kamchatka in Russia had always fascinated me as a Geographer, as it was in the far east and overlooked Alaska. Up until 1992 it was closed to Westerners. It has thirty-nine active volcanoes and hundreds of dormant ones. So on August 1st I flew out with Adventure Peaks.

We flew to Moscow and had a day sight-seeing – Red Square, Kremlin (which is huge), and St. Basil's. We got lost on the underground, but met a young Russian who took us to see the sights. Next day we flew to Petropavlovsk, the only city in Kamchatka. Kamchatka is peninsula as big as the UK and at the same latitude, but has only two roads: one going east to west and one going north for 500 kilometres and stopping. There is no road connecting to the Russian mainland! The flight was eight hours, flying over one country and eight time zones. We were in a Boeing 777 with 350 passengers, but the airport was small with one luggage conveyor belt which was overwhelmed. Our little hotel had an outdoor thermally heated pool at about forty-five degrees centigrade. Next day we boarded a six-wheeled military bus and drove towards our first volcano – Kozielskaya. A five-hour uphill walk with gear and tents. We emerged out of the cloud to a fantastic view of two volcanoes. Off at four a.m. to the summit crater which was full of ice. The entire mountain is a loose pile of rubble. Descending the crater there was a rope to hold on to, as it was steep and loose. I trod on a big block, thinking it would be safer. It shot off downhill and just missed the guide. As I got off the rope, Mike started to come down behind me and set off three big rocks, one of which hit me on the thigh! The descent after that was awful, loose rock. The last mile on the flat was through a million mosquitoes. This was definitely the worst mountain I had ever climbed.

Our main objective was to climb the highest volcano – Kluchevskaya Sopka, 4,750 metres. We had to drive 400 kilometres north on the military bus on ash roads to a small village called Kozyrievska. We stayed in huts, but there was a sauna and we had salmon caviar for starters with our meal. Next day we had to move to another hostel where we waited for three days for the weather to clear. There was nothing in the village but two basic shops, but they did sell ice cream and lots of vodka. When the weather cleared, we were taken to a helicopter airport and loaded our gear in. It was a huge military chopper. After twenty minutes we were told to get off and unload as the landing site at the volcano was a metre deep in snow! So plan B was to go on a military bus to the active volcano – Tolbachinskaya. We set off at six p.m., uphill and over rivers (no bridge) for six bumpy hours. We arrived at midnight and had to put up tents by torchlight. We woke up to find ourselves in an ash wilderness. After a little lie in we set off to explore. We soon came to a recent lava flow only three weeks old. I was the only one in the group with any geological knowledge. I showed everyone the difference between Pahoehoe and Aa. These are Hawaiian words for smooth and rough lava. We kept passing holes with hot air coming out, so we dropped a bit of paper in and it burst into flames. Water turned into steam. At one point the guide told us to stay put whilst he went to look for a lava flow. He came back after ten minutes and when he picked up his rucksack, the bottom had slightly melted! What we didn't realise was that one metre underneath our feet, the lava was still flowing. We found the end of the flow and it was moving slowly just a few feet from us. Safe, but warm!

We seemed to be in cloud, but realised it was steam from the volcano. So next day we visited it. At the bottom edge of the crater there was a six-metre-deep hole in the ground where you could see the lava flowing underneath us. The cone was just cinder rubble like a slag heap. Approaching the edge, you kept hearing whooshing sounds. It was the lava being thrown into the air every few seconds. It was being thrown thirty metres into the air and plopping back, so it was safe to descend into the crater and look into the boiling cauldron of lava. This was even more spectacular at night.

Next day we descended and drove back to Petropavlovsk to stay in a nice hotel where we had a welcome shower. Two more volcanoes the next day: Gorielaya and Tolmachova. The first was a double crater with lakes and steam vents. The other had a small glacier on it and had steam vents, solfataras, sulphur vents, boiling mud pools, and hot streams. We spent our last night at a tatty hotel and went for a four-hour boat trip in the harbour, hoping to see a Steller's sea eagle, but we didn't.

Back to Blighty the next day. We set off at two p.m. from Petropavlovsk and landed at a quarter past two in the afternoon. It actually took eight hours, but the plane was crossing eight time zones. Mike and I had a fish dinner and we both got food poisoning! The journey got worse in London when my train was cancelled due to "jumpers on the line". So I had to run to a crowded train from St. Pancras to Sheffield. Home at six p.m. and started to pack for tomorrow's trip!

Isle of Wight. We had never been to the Isle of Wight, so we booked a B&B at Totland near the Needles. The island is pretty but overcrowded and overpriced. We did see red squirrels though, outside our bedroom window.

When we got back, I went to the doc's to see about my lump that had got bigger. Another scan showed it had enlarged and got more dense. I was sent to a specialist who said it will be better if we remove it, as we don't know what it is. Three weeks later I had a minor operation to remove it. They said to come back in three weeks. Ten days later I was summoned back to the hospital to see another specialist – an oncologist. The lump was cancerous, he said. I didn't bat an eyelid at this. I don't know why, 'cos I'm not brave. He said I'd be alright. Then I went to Hull for a CT scan. The results were good. No pathogens, but he did say I had kidney and gall stones, but that was no problem! I was then sent to a third specialist who said he was going to operate again to remove any tissue that might be contaminated. So a second op. I was told, no climbing, cycling, or running for six weeks. I asked if

I could weight train in a seated position and he reluctantly agreed. Since then, I have had an MRI scan every year and up until now I'm okay. I'm keeping my fingers crossed!

2014: Only four trips this year. In March I took four of the club to Calpe in the Costa Blanca as none of them had climbed here before. We got a five-seater car very cheaply and found the Turmolina high-rise hotel also very cheaply as March is out of season. We were on the thirteenth floor with a great view of the Penon, a 1,000-feet rock jutting out to sea. We all climbed it in a couple of hours, sharing it with hundreds of yellow legged gulls that were nesting up there. They were not pleased to see us! We did the whole Bernia ridge the next day – my second time. On the rock climb there is a knife-edged ridge, one-metre thick at the top with a thirty-metre drop on one side and ten-metre drop on the other. It makes for a spectacular picture.

June and Bolivia. As a geographer I was fascinated with places on the map like Lake Titicaca, which is the highest navigable lake in the world. I flew from Heathrow, which I hate, to Miami airport, which is too big. It was twenty-eight centigrade at Miami. When we landed at La Paz it was minus one centigrade at midnight. La Paz is the world's highest capital at 12,000 feet. The airport is another 1,000 feet up! Visitors usually feel the effect of the altitude, which the locals call "soroche". The city is in a large basin and like many is overcrowded with permanent traffic jams. We never found a good restaurant and there were no pubs. However, our posh hotel served excellent food and had a good bar. Before we were let onto the mountains we had to acclimatise, so we went to Lake Titicaca. On a small ferry to the Isla del Sol where we stopped at Cococabana! We were 14,000 feet up, but we felt like we were at the seaside as there was a beach, pubs, and restaurants. We sat on the upper terrace of a beach bar and watched the sun set behind the snow-covered peaks. We met a local guide the next day and walked the length of the island, passing a stone slab where they sacrificed virgins! We caught a boat back and went for a cheap, but good, meal.

We drove back towards La Paz, but stopped at a small track and waited for our guide. An hour's drive over grassland covered in Llamas to a mule camp, where our gear was loaded onto mules. We then walked up to Base Camp and pitched our tents. Rowlando was our guide and Anna was our cook. We had a big tent to eat in with tables and chairs that the mules brought up. Behind the cook tent, the cook dumped the food waste behind a rock. We saw a strange animal eating it and asked the guide what it was. He said it was a rabbit, but it had a long tail and was grey. We found out later it was a Viscacha. Next day we went up to a ridge at 4,700 metres and down one of the best screes I have ever seen. I ran/skied down it! Pico Blanco the next day, which meant crossing a glacier and many crevasses to reach a steep snow slope up to the top. We really needed two axes here. When we got back a young lady in traditional dress approached us holding a bag. She was saying, "Cola o cerveza". She had walked up an hour from the mule camp to sell us drinks!

We were told to pack our bags for tomorrow as we were getting up at 3.30 a.m. We got to the top of the glacier by sunrise to see the pyramidal peak of Pico Mayo. One of our group, Pete, said, "I'm not going up that!"

We had to take our crampons off to descend 100 feet of rocky scree and then put them back on to ascend a steep arete (knife edge) of snow. Luckily it was hard 'neve' and very safe. A fantastic looking mountain.

Back to La Paz and the hotel so that we could climb Pitosi, a 6,000-metre peak the other side of the city. After a two-hour bumpy ride we set off uphill for three hours to the refuge. Up at one-thirty in the morning and off in an hour for a four-hour trek in the dark. After crossing a bergschrund, it got excessively windy. Al's hands and feet were cold, Pete was knackered, and I was feeling the onset of hypothermia. We were only half an hour from the top, but the guide decided to go down. We met Will coming up with the other guide, but they also retreated. We packed the next day to fly to Santa Cruz, where had to get off for ninety minutes whilst they refuelled. The plane couldn't take off fully fuelled at 13,000 feet! After a meal on the plane I felt unwell with a stomach upset and had to travel back sitting as close to a toilet as I could! Not a pleasant return journey!

Montenegro was part of Serbia until 2006 when it became independent. Joan and I booked a beach holiday at Budva. Good beaches and restaurants as expected, but our entry to the country is worth a story. We flew to Dubrovnik, as Montenegro doesn't have a big airport. We were the only ones on the plane going to Budva. We were picked up in a private car with a driver who spoke little English. At the Croatian border we showed our passports, but there was a half-mile of no-man's land and a half-mile queue! The driver got on his phone and proceeded to pass the whole queue. We got to the next border and his mates looked at our passports and waved us through! We then had to go round a huge fiord-like inlet which looked miles round. There was a ferry at a narrow point and another long queue. The driver got on his phone again and jumped to the head of the queue and we were first on! On the way into Budva there was another queue, but the driver went the back way and missed it. I gave him a good tip. There were very few Brits here, but the country is worth visiting with places like Kotor, which has a magnificent moated castle. There are lots of Serbs and Russians here and lots of thunder storms. The young folk are all fit and slim. No fat girls, just gorgeous ones! The young men all play water polo and all are good swimmers with good physiques. Food and drink was all good. There was also a beer called Niksicko!

My American friend Kyle, whom I had met on Ama Dablam, had now moved to Spain and married a Spanish girl and was now living in Seville. In December I flew out to stay with him for a week, cycling, climbing, and walking. The city is historic and beautiful, as are all Spanish cities. Even in December it was warm in the day, but cool at night. Even so, the night life is full on. People still eating and drinking in the street bars in the cold until late at night. Kyle is a top skier and moved to Granada the next year to be nearer the Sierra Nevada, which actually means snowy mountains.

2015: Provence, Corsica, and the Azores. Club trip to Provence. We stayed at Six-four les Plage, near Toulon. It was Easter and packed, but the crags were deserted and the climbing okay.

GR 20 Corsica. GR means Grande Randonnee or big tour. It is a famous route almost the length of Corsica, following the mountainous granite spine of the island. Our guide was called Coralie, who was my first female guide. There were three Brits and three Aussies also on the team. It usually takes two weeks to complete, but we only had twelve days, so we missed the first and last days. Our big bags were carried round by van to some of our stops, but could not reach many of them as there are few roads across Corsica. If there was a road, we stayed at a gite and if no road, we camped. The tents were pop-up tents and sleeping mats provided. This meant light rucksacks. The first day was through granite spires. Where descents were too steep, chains were fixed to hold onto. Each day was different. Wooded valleys, rocky ridges, peaks, lakes, streams with pools, and always views to either coast. Alpine choughs circled down when we stopped, as they know that when walkers stop, they get food out. They were almost tame! The route is very popular and most campsites were full. We met a German guy who was doing it by himself, carrying all his food, tent and cooking gear. The penultimate day was to the Cirque de Solitude, which is notoriously steep and rocky. Unfortunately, the week before, a thunderstorm had hit it and released a snow pack and caused a rock avalanche, which buried and killed five people. The authorities then closed the route forever. Some walking groups were picked up by coach and taken around it. Coralie thought our group could walk around it on a steep and long bypass. We got up at four o'clock and walked in the dark for an hour to a col and traversed the mountain. We finished up in Bastia to a great lunch in the sun. Corsica is not visited by many Brits, but is great if you like a quiet, scenic holiday.

Azores. Another venue, rarely visited by Brits. Nine islands in the middle of the Atlantic, owned by the Portuguese. The only international airport is on Sao Miguel at Porto Delgada. All the other islands are connected by ferry or light aircraft. We flew to the island of Pico, which has the biggest volcano on it and is the highest point in Portugal at 7,000 feet. As with all volcanic islands, there are no sandy beaches. Our hotel had a big swimming pool, but the locals had built sea pools in the rocky inlets. We hired a car to drive to the volcano, but there was a storm and the cloud ceiling was 1000 feet and we couldn't see anything, so we drove right around the island. The nearest island was Faial, which had frequent ferries. Up until 1947 the islands were still whaling. The whaling station here was now a museum and well worth a visit. We drove to the big crater in the middle of the island, which is five kilometres around the crest. At the other end of the island is the most recently active cone, which exploded in 1947 and buried many houses in ash. They wouldn't let you climb Pico without a guide, so I joined a small group and went up. You can drive up half way, so the climb was only 3,000 feet and very easy. You couldn't get lost if you tried. On the top you can feel hot air coming out of the cracks.

I managed to persuade Joan to go on a whale spotting boat, as it was a big rubber power craft and didn't wallow like a big ship. She got sea sick on a big boat in Tenerife once. It was flat calm this day, no problem. We saw dolphins, Cory's shearwaters, and then three Sperm whales. I even got a shot of its tail as it dived. If you ever go, visit other islands as they are all different.

2016: Costa Rica, Kalymnos, K2, Costa Blanca, Ann-Mare's marriage, and becoming a great-grandad. And my 70th birthday. In 2015 Natalie had a daughter called Alyssa – our first great-grandchild! In 2016 Adele had a daughter, Aaliyah, and then Cheryl had Alice. Three great-grandchildren in a year!

Costa Rica. We went in February which is the drier season. Two seven-hour trips via New York to San Jose. It's an old fogie trip. We felt young! We drove over the mountains to the Caribbean coast.

We stopped for breakfast and saw a sloth in a tree, much to Joan's delight. We then transferred to a small boat to Tortuguero, which is in the coastal jungle, and stayed in a hut with no windows, just a fine anti-insect mesh. There are no roads here. Travel is all by boat. The water is warm, but full of cayman! Howler monkeys woke us up at four in the morning. On the way to breakfast, we saw sloths, iguanas, humming birds, a basilisk, and the guide saw a boa constrictor slither under somebody's hut! Tortuguero means turtle bay and they are everywhere. A boat trip is magic for bird and animal watching. We saw herons, kingfishers, jacanas, parrots, woodpeckers, turtles, and cayman. The boatman spotted a cayman and we went photograph it. I couldn't see it at first, as it was camouflaged in the weed and floating wood. We were three feet away from it!

Next day a bus trip to La Fortuna in the volcanic area. Our hotel had hot volcanic springs made into cascades with seats under water and tables just above the water. You signalled a waiter to order your beer and it was delivered. So you sit in warm water and drink cold beer! Luxury! At breakfast the hotel had a bird-feeding station which attracted hundreds of birds, which were used to tourists. Before going to Arenal volcano we had the chance to swim in a waterfall pool, which was surprisingly warm.

Next to Monteverde cloud forest. Outside our hotel somebody was feeding a coati. Our guide reported them as you are not to feed the wild animals. It is a strict Costa Rican law to protect all animals. In this forest we went for a meal, but were taught to make a chicken tortilla. Outside coatis and white-faced capuchins waited for scraps. The forest was full of butterflies and birds like the blue crowned motmot. We went back to San Jose for a meal before we flew home. Costa Rica is a fantastic country and very different to the other South and Central American countries as the government is dedicated to wildlife, education, and eco-tourism. In 1948, a new government disbanded the army in favour of education for all. American and European tourists are the mainstay of the economy, along with bananas and coffee.

May saw the climbing club back in Kalymnos for a week's rock climbing, eating, and drinking – as usual!

K2. This is the second highest mountain in the world. It is not near Everest, but in the Pakistani Karakorum. This trip was not on the previous year, due to political unrest, but I got a place last minute this year, so I booked it. Then my wife asked when it was. When I told her, she said, "So you'll be away on the first of August – Ann-Marie's wedding day."

Whoops! All flights to the Himalaya go via Doha. It was thirty-three centigrade at midnight! We then flew to Islamabad and stayed in the Islamabad hotel. It is a Muslim country and that means no alcohol for a month! How will I survive? On arrival a waiter brought out a big tray of drinks that looked like beer. It was chilled lemon tea! There were twelve of us, including the leader – all Brits. We had a day in Islamabad and went to see the main mosque, which is huge. We were the only westerners there, as the city is not a tourist destination. The locals were fascinated and kept asking us for selfies with them. Fame at last. Next day we flew north to Skardhu. There was torrential rain on the way to the airport. I expected a small plane like we had in Kathmandu, but it was a full-sized jet. We sat on the runway and the pilot said they were waiting for a spare part. Twenty minutes later, no spare part. So the pilot said, "I think we'll be okay, God willing," and took off.

We flew into the upper Indus valley flying low between the mountain peaks. Then a bumpy ride into Skardhu, which is a scruffy town with an unmade dusty road lined with garages, fuel depots, motor bike shops, and nothing else. Once in the hotel we went looking for a shoe shop to buy some sandles for me. I got a pair for seven pounds. On the way back, Melvyn and I bought an ice cream. I mentioned it to the guide.

"Was it a wrapped one?"

We said no. It was probably home made with local water. You may get the runs. We did!!

Next day we walked up to the castle overlooking the Indus river. Very hot. Then it was time to move onto the trail. This meant a seven-hour drive in Toyota Land Cruisers. After two hours on proper roads, we got stopped by the army. We had to show our passports even though we were still in Pakistan. It was hot in the cars as they had no air con. So I was wearing sandals, a vest, and shorts. As I presented my passport to the army bloke, he looked up at me and said, "You have nice body, are you a body builder?"

Well, the lads cracked up laughing! We were then off road and the landscape changed from farming to a river valley lined with mountain sides of glacial boulder clay, which is very unstable. It was raining when we suddenly stopped and were told to get out, put on our helmets and run! The unstable rock had avalanched and taken the road out! We ran, dodging the falling rocks. Our gear was taken from the jeeps by the porters and we jumped in another jeep on the other side. Another hair-raising ride to Askole, the last village. Our gear arrived and the porters put up the tents. There was one shop in the village called the Askole shopping centre. It was a small hut with no lights inside! A little boy followed me asking questions in the local tongue. I gave him some sweets which seemed to please him.

In the morning, about 100 porters lined up and were bossed about by the soldier in charge. The porters took all the camping gear and were wearing flip flops or sandals. Mules and donkeys carried the heavy gear. We followed the river that drained the Baltoro glacier and stopped at good campsites with toilets. The path often came very close to the river, which was a raging torrent. You could hear the boulders crunching along the river bed. On arrival at one campsite, we were told that a mule had fallen in and was swept away with William's gear on and some tents. They recovered the mule's body and all the gear. William's gear was completely soaked and had to be hung up to dry. Some porters were walking with goats and some carrying chickens. There are no fridges, so this was fresh meat! That night we had goat meatballs. On the third day we saw the great Boltoro glacier. It was black and covered in millions of tons of rock and boulders. Walking on it was tough, as it was loose and in giant piles. Up and down all day for five days. Every half mile or so there would be a valley glacier joining the Boltoro, bringing more rock and ice. As we got further up the rock on the surface became less thick and we could see more ice. The mountains either side were incredible towers of granite, like the Trango Tower and the Cathedral. After six days trekking we arrived at Concordia where three glaciers meet. From now on we camped on the ice and not on the valley sides. We had our first sight of K2!

I was still having trouble with my bowels and couldn't shake off the Delhi belly! Not good when staying in a tent. We eventually camped at K2 base camp. Within an hour of arriving, a huge avalanche came off K2 and swept right across the Goodwin-Austin glacier! I was one of four to climb the Kharut pyramid the next day, but I was in no state to climb with a harness on with diarrhoea! The group tried the climb, but the conditions were too dangerous to summit. We met a group of Brits that had just come off K2 as their Camp Three had been wiped out by avalanche, taking a load of their gear, but fortunately no life was lost. There is a memorial near to the base camp which has the names of all the climbers killed on K2. There were a lot, including Alison Hargreaves who was lost with twelve others in a storm many years ago.

It snowed the day we started to return, but at Concordia camp the porters revolted as we were going to go back over a high snowy pass at night. They all had mobiles and had seen a storm approaching and refused to ascend in a storm at night in sandals. I don't blame them!! So we had to return the same way, but with longer walks. On the last day before we reached Askole, two Landrovers picked us up and gave us a lift into the village. Another hairy ride back in the jeeps, but we still had to walk across the landslide. On arrival back at Skardu, we heard that out flight back to Islamabad had been cancelled due to bad weather. If the pilots can't see the landing strip or mountains, they are not allowed to fly! Plan B was to go over the Karakorum highway which we were told we could not do as it was too dangerous. But we had to. Two days driving on awful roads to Islamabad, where we had a bath and big meal. Still no alcohol until we got on the plane. Wine has never tasted so good. When I got back, my bowels were still bad, so I went to the doctor's and took a sample. Two days later I went back and he said it was just traveller's tummy. I had had it for three weeks and had lost five kilos. I don't have five spare kilos and had lost a lot of muscle. I told him I was running a half marathon in seven weeks' time, so I need to put back some muscle. He suggested steak and eggs. So, I had that every lunch as well as a big tea. I put back three kilos in two weeks and started running. The Birmingham half marathon was five days after my seventieth birthday. As my birthday was a Monday, I had a big party at my house on the Saturday. It was twelve hours long, from midday to midnight. The next day a I ran a training thirteen miles, despite a hangover. I travelled over to Birmingham to stay with Addie, who was running with me. I say with me, as I was forty minutes faster than her. I finished in a disappointing one hour forty minutes, but I was the fastest in my age group by fifty minutes. I had beaten 18,500 other runners all younger than me.

Joan and I finished the year by going to the Costa Blanca and staying in a quiet resort called La Marina. It was early October and no kids about. We took my mate Pete for a big paella. He was surprised and pleased to see us.

2017: No big mountains this year. Just two climbing trips and three holidays with Joan. She was seventy in November this year. We decided on a spring holiday in Tenerife. We stayed at Puerto de Santiago, near Los Gigantes. A pool holiday, but I get bored, so I hired a racing bike and cycled up to the nearest town in the mountains. After fifty metres on the road there was a sixteen-per-cent gradient out of town! Then the next fifteen kilometres were ten per cent. A tough start. There is a road up towards Teide, the big volcano, which is twenty kilometres long, so I went up the next day. I overtook a Brit who was less fit than me! After fifteen kilometres the temperature went up to twenty-five centigrade with no shade. Too much, so I headed back down. I had a helmet camera on, so I raced down and only one car overtook me, as it was so bendy.

Kalymnos in May again. Brilliant climbing, food, drink, and company. I did thirty-five routes. Fingers get very sore as the skin is worn thin. You don't realise until you pick up a hot or very cold drink. I went back to Kalymnos again in October with a different group of climbers and did forty-five routes. I did more as I was climbing with Colin, a very fit forty-year-old past pupil. It was my seventy-first birthday on this trip. Colin and I went on the ferry to Telendos with Colin's dad, Simon and John, our climbing doctor. We walked for an hour uphill to a 900-foot climb called Wild Country. It was nine pitches long and took us two-and-a-half hours, climbing in the sun. My feet were killing me. Then a ninety-minute walk off around the other coast. We were greeted with a bar selling cold beers. So we stayed for dinner before the ferry back. A great day for my seventy-first.

I took Joan to Italy as we hadn't been there before. We stayed in Puglia on the Adriatic coast. We normally book bed and breakfast and then eat out. We didn't realise that this hotel was mainly full board and nobody went out. There were no restaurants nearby. It was a twenty-Euro taxi-ride to the nearest village. So we went to a little supermarket to buy some food for the evening, and we also pinched food from breakfast! We did find a little family-run restaurant near the hotel beach, but had to book it, as it was end of season. We were saved. One trip to Alberobello, which is a world heritage site, for having conical-roofed limestone houses.

Joan was seventy in November, so Ann-Marie, her husband Adonis, and I took her to Budapest to visit the Christmas market. November in Hungary is not good for weather. It rained, snowed, and was sunny, but cold on the last day. But a lovely, clean, and friendly city.

2018. Five trips this year – Patagonia, Alicante, Kalymnos, Madrid, Leonidio, and Mum's 100th birthday! Dave went with me on the trip to Patagonia. It's the first time anyone has come with me from home, but he had just retired. A long trip. Manchester to Heathrow, then Santiago and Punta Arenas. The girl at Manchester said our luggage would go straight through, but it was taken off at Santiago and had to go through customs again. Our pick-up at Punta Arenas never turned up, so we had to take a taxi to a hotel. Next day we were driven for three hours to Puerto Natales, were we had a meal and went to the pub. Another two hours to Eco camp. On the way we saw guanacos, rheas, caracals, and flamingos at the road side. At camp we met the rest: two Aussies, an Irishman, and six American girls. I was a bit depressed at the number of women, as they usually hold us up! However, the American girls were all very fit. We were camping in big dome tents which were already set up and always on wooden pallets as the ground was always wet. It rains a lot in Patagonia as we were about to find out. First day was a twenty-mile walk to Dickson Camp. On the way we saw a condor, ibis, and other unrecognisable birds. We woke up next morning to rain, which soon turned to snow. We walked all day in deep snow through woods. Los Perros camp was in a pine forest and the snow kept falling on the tent in big lumps. The campsite was a wet bog. You had to wade to the toilet and cook tent. My comfy Merrill boots were now saturated. They are old Goretex boots, but the Goretex was not now working. For the rest of the trip I had to put on soaking boots every morning!

It had stopped snowing the next day, but we had to go over a 1,400-metre pass in deep snow. At the top was a view of the Grey Glacier, which was a small arm of the great Patagonian glacier. Our camp was Refugio Grey. We camped, but ate at a big hotel full of people that hadn't walked there. The meal was good, but the beer and shower were better. We only had to walk for three hours next day, so we went to see the icebergs in the lake. It was very windy, but dry.

Gales and rain all night, followed by rain and gales all day! The wind was blowing up big waves on the lake we were walking next to and the spray from the wave tops were forming dancing rainbows. One more day to Eco Camp and yes, you've guessed it, it rained. Then the highlight of the trip was the last day, walking up to the Torres del Paine, which are three granite monoliths, 2,000 feet high. And it didn't rain!! Unfortunately, it was a bit cloudy, so the pictures were not perfect.

After a long flight back, we landed at Heathrow to be told our flight to Manchester had been cancelled, but we got on an earlier flight. We had to wait for forty-five minutes for de-icing. We landed in Manchester in a snow storm. The last flight from London that day due to snow. It was a small plane to Manchester, so not long to wait for our luggage. Dave's came first but mine never arrived. It took five days to get to me due to Pennine passes being closed. It had a week's worth of damp, smelly clothes in it!

In April Joan and I went to Alicante for some early sun. Madrid and southern Spain were having snow, but it was over twenty centigrade here. Huge beaches, but very quiet. We visited Pete again.

Two rock climbing trips this year. Kalymnos in May and Leonidio in October. Leonidio is on the Greek mainland, but is a five-hour drive from Athens. The village here is an agricultural centre at the end of a large limestone valley, which has thousands of climbs. As it is a new venue there are few places to stay and fewer restaurants and bars. Nearly all the climbs are accessed via a 500-foot scree slope. Not good! We have been spoiled by all the restaurants and bars in Kalymnos. There were eight of us on the trip and at the carousel all the luggage came off except mine! The Greek staff were most unhelpful. All my climbing gear was in it! I bought a new pair of boots and borrowed some clothes from the others. My luggage came three days later!

My Spanish group went to Madrid for the second time this year. Just four of us. We visited Toledo this time on a superb train. It had to be booked and there was no standing and no rubbish. Why aren't British trains like this? Toledo is the old capital and is sited on an incised meander like Durham. The river gorge surrounds the city as a natural defence and has massive fortified gates and a castle. It is famous for its steel swords. You can buy a suit of armour for 8,000 Euros, but I don't know how you would get it home! Wear it perhaps?

On September 1st it was my Mum's 100th birthday. We arranged a letter from the Queen, which came on the day and we had a surprise party for her. She thought she was just going for a meal with her three children. But everyone was there, including all her great-great-grandchildren. We invited the local paper, the Grimsby Telegraph, round who expected her to arrive in a wheelchair or with a walking aid. She just walked in! There were over fifty of us from all over the country. She made the front cover and was a page three girl with lots of photos.

2019. Five trips this year: Chile, Kalymnos, Pyrenees, Provence, and Italy. Ojos del Salado is the second highest mountain in the Andes at 6,908 metres. It means 'salty eyes' in Spanish. A long journey: Humberside, Amsterdam, Buenos Aires, Santiago, and Copiapo. I had an eight-hour wait in Amsterdam airport. The plane landed in Buenos Aires where we had to get off and get on again after an hour. I met the rest of the group at Santiago. Mostly Brits but two Americans and a Swedish girl. We landed on a sandy airstrip in the Atacama desert near to Copiapo, which is a small industrial town based on mining. Very hot and sunny, but no air con at our basic hotel. We were driven in three Toyota Land Cruisers to a grassy campsite at 3,000 metres. We went up a scree slope to 4,000 metres as a warm-up. Next day was a long drive on a deserted road to Laguna St. Rosa at 4,000 metres. As we left the town a sign read, "last petrol for 200kms". The road had no villages, farms,cafes, petrol stations, or anything. This campsite had a salt lake full of flamingos, but also had some huts. For a small fee we could use the huts instead of camping. That's for me! Everyday started the same. Blue skies and calm. By noon it was blowing a gale. We ascended a mountain called Seven Hermanas at 4,950 metres in a gale. Next day we climbed Pastallitos at 5,100 metres. It was scree all the way up and down. All the mountains here are piles of scree and virtually no solid rock. There are no trees or vegetation anywhere.

We then drove to Laguna Verde, which was surrounded by cliffs of pumice. The lake is green as it has arsenic in it. At the edge of the lake there was a desiccated cow that had obviously drank from the lake. Just before we got to the lake there was a road sign showing a waterfall. There was a small river with a small waterfall – in the middle of the driest desert in the world. We had a dawn start the day after, up a long ridge. Scree again. I gave up at the end of a ridge as my breathing was holding me back. Several others also gave up. We came down through several fields of penitents, which seem to be found only in South America. I had been first up the first three summits, but I was struggling with my breathing and had developed a cough.

A long drive the next day to Base Camp for the summit. All sand. The base camp is at 5,200 metres which is higher than Everest Base Camp. I found it hard to sleep at this height. I got out at five a.m. for a wee. I stood outside in bare feet at 5,200 metres and at minus five centigrade I didn't feel cold as the air is so dry and there is no frost! The sky was fantastic. The Milky Way was ablaze and the stars seemed massive. We all walked up to the upper camp the next day at 5,800 metres. Nick, Jim, and I went up slowly with Carrie, the Scottish guide. My breathing and cough were holding me back and I was really struggling to keep going. Nick and I decided not to summit the next day as we didn't think we could do it. So six went up at midnight. Three turned back and three made it.

After a long drive back to Copiapo, we had a day to relax. To get back to the airport we stayed at Bahia des Ingles, a seaside resort that looked like an English resort, with lots of bars and restaurants. We stayed at the best hotel in town with its own pool. A bit of luxury at last.

Kalymnos in May yet again. It is always good here. We ate on the second evening at Panos, the restaurant next to the hotel and eight of us had a meal with two litres of wine for eighty-five Euros!! It's no wonder we keep going back!

Pyrenees. Coralie, the French guide who had led my GR 20 trip in 2015, e-mailed me to say she had started her own company. So I thought I would join her for a trip to the Pyrenees, which I had never climbed. I booked a flight to Toulouse via Humberside and Amsterdam. There were only thirty minutes between landing in Amsterdam and taking off to Toulouse! Luckily there were only a few folk on the plane from Humberside and the pilot took off early and arrived early, giving me more time to find my way in this big airport. I was worried that my luggage might not be transferred in such a short time, so I asked a hostess to check if my luggage was on, as all my climbing gear was in it. Unlike Leonidio, it was on. I got a bus to the railway station, which was packed. The train was a double-decker and almost empty. I had booked an Air bed and breakfast in Montrejeau. I found the road, but there wasn't a number eighteen. I asked at a garage and they didn't know, so they rang the lady in question, who came to fetch me in her car. Her number eighteen was a big block of flats with no number on! And her flat was number nineteen. Confusing? I walked into town and it was closed (Sunday), except for a bar and a pizza place. I wasn't meeting the rest until four p.m. the next day. Monday was market day and the town was alive, with lots of bars and restaurants. I met the rest of the crew at the station and we drove off over the border to Spain. We were staying in alpine huts and you only needed a sheet sleeping bag, as bedding was provided. I had never stayed in alpine huts before and was impressed with the food and accommodation.

Day one, to Cap de Llauset hut. We left the road and went up a very steep path through a forest for an hour. I thought I was going to die! As we came out of the trees it got really hot and I asked for a drink stop. Coralie said we would stop at the lake. Coralie and two of the blokes went in for a swim. Coralie swam right across the lake! Afterwards everybody had thought the same about the first hour. It hurt everyone. I think Coralie was testing us all. The hut looked like something from space. It gleamed in the sun. Stainless steel and solar panels. As you entered there was a boot room and a selection of Crocs to wear. We went straight to the bar and had a couple of beers. Our room had two double bunks and an en-suite toilet and shower. The three-course meal was also superb.

Next say was easier. We passed Aneto, which is the highest peak in the Pyrenees. Then a boring walk down a rough road to Benasque, the only town we meet. We stayed at the mountain school, which had its own climbing wall. Benasque is Spain's Chamonix and is full of bars, restaurants, and climbing shops. Coralie bought me a walking pole as I don't like them, but needed one for the steep descents. A French couple in the group decided to leave us here as it was too much for them and this was the only road that would allow them to get back. Deep into the mountains next day to Angel Orus, which was full of noisy Spaniards. It was now hot and sunny with stunning scenery. On to the next hut at Biados, four of us detoured to Posets, the second highest peak in the Pyrenees at 3,369 metres, only thirty five metres short of Aneto. A rocky ascent with a big patch of hard snow in a gully. The valley down to Soula Hut was like a Swiss valley with cows with bells around their necks. We were now in hydro electric power country. Soula was a power station and the route from it was a well-engineered footpath up to a feeder reservoir. I was in shorts and a vest. At the reservoir the wind got up, so I put a jacket on. We crossed several small glaciers and many moraines. At the high point there was a crack of thunder and the heavens opened. We struggled to get our waterproofs on in the gale, but it didn't last long. The hut at Portillon was superb and even sold Leffe beer. My favourite!

It rained and thundered all night. In the morning we were in the cloud as we were so high. It had stopped raining, but we were almost in the cloud. We stopped at a hut for a coffee and was told that our route to Maupas was blocked by a landslide, so we had to go over a mountain ridge direct, and no path. It began to drizzle. Up through long vegetation and loose rock in the cloud and rain. Lovely!! We had lunch in a shepherd's hut to keep dry and then followed an engineer's cut on the mountainside, which was designed to catch water for a reservoir. This meant walking on a narrow piece of rock between a drop and the water cut. It was so narrow that Coralie made everyone but me walk 'in' the watercourse. She thought I would be okay as I was a climber. We then had to crawl up a steep scree slope to get to the hut. The hut was small and packed. It had old-fashioned alpine accommodation with three layers of bunks with no division between the beds. The hut had only one outside toilet for over thirty people! My close neighbours were girls on their phones all night! It's a good job I was tired and slept through it all.

Big descent the next day and back in Spain and the sun. We stopped at the Renclusa hut which serves as the start to Aneto, so it was packed, but also big and comfortable. Last day next, up two passes to a high breche and then down a never-ending valley for six scorching hours. There was no real path, lots of boulders, and thick vegetation. As we got close to the road and on a waymarked path, Coralie told us to keep going on the path and stop at the road, whilst she would hitch a lift to her van and save us three kilometres on the road back to the cars. She RAN off! By the time we got to the road she was back with her van. What a star!! My feet were on fire. Back at the hut we had two beers and Coralie dropped me back at the airport. This was at ten p.m. and my flight was at six in the morning. I had a snack and slept on the floor. Two short flights and home.

In September, ten of us went to Provence to rock climb. We stayed at luxury apartment with a pool at Vaison la Romaine, a scenic village with extensive Roman remains, near Orange. Great climbing especially on Les Dentelles, which as the name suggests are vertical teeth-like limestone crags. The rock strata has been turned ninety degrees to the vertical. On a wet day Rob and I went to the Roman amphitheatre which looks nearly new!

In October I took Joan to Sorrento for a holiday as I had heard it was worth a visit. The bus transfer was longer than the flight! Sorrento is a long narrow town with narrow streets and over fifty hotels. It is a traffic jam. Cruise ships come in every day and fill the place with Americans. I thought it would be quiet in October. Wrong. The place is beautiful but over-touristy. We had to visit Pompei and Vesuvius which we did in a day. Pompei was swamped with tourists, so I asked the guide if Vesuvius would be the same. She said no. She was wrong! The buses drive within 600 feet of the summit. There were over thirty buses and thousands of folk, walking up the cinder path. Most were struggling. There must be a lot of heart attacks here. The trip to the Amalfi coast was good, but again too many tourists. This wasn't for me! I'll stick to mountains and no people.

Ridge on Ama Dablam

Collapsed Serac

Kyle, me, Ama Dablam and Everest

Top of Ventoux

Top of Cotopaxi

2 Ladies and me

Lundy –sea stack

Alp d'Huez

Kamchatka – walking with a little sack!

Lava flow and me

Eruption at night

Bernia ridge

Pico Mayo summit – me and guide

Pico Mayo

Chough

Azores – Pico

Sperm whale tail

Costa Rico – Howler monkey

Avalanche K2

K2 and Me

Telendos – me and Colin

Torres del Paine – me and Morty

Chapter 8.

2020s: Covid takes over.

I had two trips booked. Arizona and Kalymnos. Both cancelled!! By summer things were looking better so I contacted Coralie about her Mercantour trip in the French/Italian Alps. It was touch and go, but eventually it went. I would not fly, so I drove there. Seven a.m. ferry to Calais and stopped at Dijon to find a hotel. I found a small, strange place that was having a rock and roll disco for old fogies!! No restaurants or bars open as it was a Sunday. More motorway to Grenoble where the mountains begin. Now it's all fantastic scenery. I got to Briancon by dinner and a pleasant hotel. Briancon is the highest town in France at 4,000 feet. It has a magnificent castle and beautiful views. I met Coralie for a drink in the evening as she lived in a village 1,000 feet above Briancon. The Col d'Izoard is south of Briancon and is a major col in the Tour de France. There were hundreds of cyclists cycling up it as a challenge. I did it when I was eighteen. Then over the Col du Vars to the village of Larche, just below Col de Larche. I met the rest of the team here, Coralie, Sevrine, and Cyril. The same group as last year in the Pyrenees.

Off at six a.m. By dinner Coralie decided to do an extra summit. Only an extra 1,000 feet. No path, just awful, steep scree. Sevrine fell over and did a somersault! When I got to the top I noticed that I was bleeding. I had gashed my shin and not noticed. I had decided to wear my new waterproof, lightweight boots that I had worn in. After one day, both my big toe nails hurt, even though they were not a tight fit! We walked for ten hours. My Fitbit said I'd done 43,000 steps, 399 staircases, and used 4,000 calories. The Mercantour is the French side of the Maritime Alps and follows the Italian border. For the first few days we were in Italy. I had forgotten that in World War Two, France and Italy were enemies. The border had many pill boxes, forts, and military roads. The terrain was always rocky and we crossed up to three cols a day. I began to fall behind on the descents as my toes hurt and then I developed a blister on my heel. I have never had a blister for years. A couple of days later my right ankle began to hurt when I went downhill, especially on rough ground.

Each day we walked for eight to ten hours over rocky cols with steep descents. Descending became a nightmare for me. At one hut there were lots of ibex that were almost tame. We also saw mouflon, chamois, vultures, and alpine choughs. Descending to the Merveilles hut we passed some Bronze Age rock engravings and some spectacular glacial rock striations. We can now see the Mediterranean Sea and Corsica. We climb the Cime du Diable at 2,685 metres and descend to a road (at last) and a ski hut for a free, hot shower and brilliant meal. The penultimate day we have a 1,500-metre descent to Sospel, which took three-and-a-half hours. Then two large, cold beers in the town square!

To get back to the cars we had to take a train through the mountains to Italy. The original idea was to walk to Menton then get a train to Nice on a Saturday. I had noticed before I set off to France that the Tour de France was racing from Nice up the road we were going to be driving up! Coralie did not know about this, even though a French! Plan B was to miss out the last day and go through Italy. It rained heavily this day, soaking the cyclists. We drove through the clouds and got back to our cars. I drove back to Briancon and stayed at a small gite in Puy St. Andre. It rained all the next day as I drove back. I stopped at Rheims to find a hotel and drove round the city and didn't see one! I carried on to the next town to find a hotel. Nothing except a strange basic one in a business park. It was full! So I had a meal and a few drinks and slept in the car. Only two hours from Calais and was home by tea. Then two weeks of self isolation!

October 12th marked fifty years of Joan and I being together. So I booked a long weekend at a Warner holiday hotel. It was Thoresby Hall near Sherwood Forest. Three nights of luxury food, drink, and entertainment. There are no children at these places, just old fogies like us! Lots to do. Walking in the beautiful grounds, archery, and falconry. There are bars, spars, wine tasting, and an indoor pool. My highlight was the falconry with peregrine falcons, gyr falcons, and several type of owls.

This year had been difficult for my sister and me, in looking after Mother. We were cooking her meals and making sure she had enough to eat, but her short-term memory was failing. So we organised two carers to come in, one in the morning and one in the evening. She didn't like them visiting and tore up their notes! She wasn't washing properly and wasn't changing her clothes. We got more help in, but then she kept falling over and the helpers were not allowed to pick her up, so they rang me to do it. We had a fall alarm fitted on her wrist, but she kept taking it off. After many discussions with the authorities, I decided we would have to put her in a home. Many were full or had Covid. One of Joan's friends, Angie, worked in a home and we got her in after a covid test. My mother had always said she wasn't going into a home, as she wanted to die in house she was born in! My sister and I eventually took her to the home saying we were taking her to a private hospital for a check-up. Within three hours they sent us a picture of her in clean clothes with her hair washed and tidy. She soon realised she was in a home, but quite liked it, as it was en-suite and warm. She has now put on weight, looks much better, and has never fallen over.

Then lockdown and a poor Christmas. What will happen in 2021? We can now see Mum face to face and she is fine and 103 in September.

We also had another great-grandchild in September 2020: Natalie gave birth to Evalin.

Mum's 100th. -Birthday girl

Penitentes – Atacama

Top of Posets – Pyrenees

Summit – Mercantour with Coralie, Sev and Cyril

Ibex

Acknowledgements.

To Mum and Dad who brought me up properly.

To my wife Joan who has put up with me for fifty years.

To the Haven Gym weight-lifting club who trained me to national level.

To Lindsey climbing club where I made many friends and climbed with all over Europe.

To Adventure Peaks, Mountain Professionals and Coralie who guided me on the big mountains.

Printed in the United States
by Baker & Taylor Publisher Services